Wit & Wisdom

A Treasury of International Quotations

William Davis

Adam was the only man who, when he said a good thing, knew that nobody had said it before him.

Mark Twain

If they haven't heard it before, it's original.

Gene Fowler

I might repeat to myself, slowly and soothingly, a list of quotations beautiful from minds profound; if I can remember any of the damn things.

Dorothy Parker

There is no reason why a book of quotations should be dull; it has its uses in idleness as well as in study.

HL Mencken

No-one is exempt from talking nonsense; the misfortune is to do it solemnly.

Montaigne

Wit is the sudden marriage of ideas which before their union were not perceived to have any relation.

Mark Twain

He is no wise man who cannot play the fool upon occasion.

Thomas Fuller

My method is to take the utmost trouble to find the right thing to say, and then to say it with the utmost levity.

George Bernard Shaw

Introduction

Business life would be dull without wit. It helps to establish personal rapport; defuses anger; provokes reflection as well as laughter; pricks pomposity; and plays a key role in making social events enjoyable.

You may be one of those fortunate people who are endowed with a natural talent for wit. If so, congratulations. But there is no reason why we should expect everyone in business to have that gift. Many of us don't.

We have all witnessed the desperate attempts of others to be funny, especially when faced with the daunting task of speaking after dinner. They approach with a haggard look. "I've got to make this speech. Do you know any stories?" They go off fortified with some terrible old lemon, make a hopeless mess of it, and wait for the laugh that doesn't come before continuing, as scripted, "but seriously...". Agony all round.

Telling jokes is not the same as being witty. Few things are more embarrassing than having to listen to people who think they are in the same league as professional comedians. They string together a series of jokes without any regard for the context or relevance and are surprised to find that they die a silent death. The art of the humorous speech is that it *remains* a speech, moulded to the theme of the event with every remark pertinent to the

Introduction

occasion. So long as humour has a point, a sense of direction and is unlikely to offend, you will never be far off target.

Particular care needs to be taken when one is asked to speak to a foreign audience. A joke that works well at home may misfire in another country, either because it is not understood or because people find it offensive. One should certainly avoid anything to do with race or ethnic minorities.

During my years as the editor of *Punch* I made annual speaking tours of the United States. I quickly discovered that Americans, as a rule, do not like to hear foreigners joking about their habits and institutions, or even about their politicians. It is far better to poke fun at your own foibles. Americans are by no means alone in this: others, including the British, also tend to react unfavourably when a foreigner makes jokes at their expense. Self-denigration is the key to being liked by an audience.

There are, of course, occasions when humour of any sort is inappropriate. If one is asked to make a presentation on a serious topic, early in the day, attempts to be funny are liable to fall flat - worse, they may well detract from the message you want to get across. You may be witty, but you stand to lose the credit of being sensible.

As a professional speaker I take a great deal of trouble to find out about the aims of an event, the people I will be addressing, and what is expected of me. I do my best to avoid unnecessary jargon, useless padding, and repetition. A good speech should be soundly constructed, persuasive, and delivered with confidence. I am always a little nervous - everyone is - but I try not to show it. An

Introduction

audience does not want to see you ill-at-ease.

I have a tendency to speak rather fast in normal life, but I have learned to curb it when I speak in public. Humour is always the one ingredient of a speech where racing speed shows up at its worst. Timing is all-important. One should never speak into a laugh or rush headlong from one aspect to another without giving the audience time to digest the previous information.

It helps if you don't read a speech - I prefer to use cue cards - but careful preparation is essential. I usually draft out in note form all the salient points I want to include and then construct the speech as a complete "story". The first and last sentences are crucial. You must create rapport and catch their interest right from the start. You can then launch into your subject. Don't end too abruptly or with a lame sentence like "well, that's all I've got to say" or "I see that my time is up". Never say "in conclusion" and then ramble on for another ten minutes. Thank the audience for their attention, tell them how much you have enjoyed being there, and wish them every success in the future. Some speakers also like to finish with a joke. Here is one that has worked for me:

"I'm going to quit before I end up like the mediaeval knight who returned home to his castle in very poor shape. He was bruised and battered. His armour was dented in a dozen places, and he was practically falling off his horse.

When the king came out to greet him, he asked the knight what on earth had happened to him. The knight said: 'My lord, I merely went out to talk to your enemies in the west'. The king said: 'But I don't have any enemies

Introduction

in the west'. The knight said: 'Well, now you do!'
I'm going to sit down before I make any more enemies."

This is a book of quotations, so you will find very few jokes or anecdotes. It is intended for the quick collaring of an apt reference and also for browsing: it can help to spice up your material and, I hope, will also be entertaining to read. Many busy people don't have time to dig around for suitable quotes. I have often felt the need for such a book myself, especially when I have had to speak at short notice. I have called it *Business Life Wit & Wisdom* because I wanted to include advice and comments from people whose opinions I respect.

I like quotations because they have the merit of being short - "brevity is the soul of wit". They can be used to supercharge your conversation, your speeches, or your writing at the right time. They are often a handy substitute for a sentiment or opinion that we ourselves would not dare to utter. I have tried to avoid the pompous, but some may well strike you as being rather pretentious. It is a risk that I felt able to take.

Some will also be familiar. You may have seen or heard them elsewhere, especially if they came from renowned wits like Oscar Wilde, Mark Twain, or George Bernard Shaw. Many quotations are old friends whose existence we are glad to be reminded of; others are new friends whose acquaintance we are glad to make. Always acknowledge your source when quoting well-known people; you don't really need to bother with unknowns.

Remember that the quotations expressed by authors (some taken out of context) are not necessarily their own beliefs. Many novelists and playwrights, even poets, put

Introduction

into the mouths of characters thoughts and sentiments different, even contrary, to their own. It should also be kept in mind that many have been originally spoken or written in an age quite different from the one we know today.

One of the challenges for the ingenious user of a book like this is the task of adaptation. Change them around whichever way you like. Make them your own. Edit, shape, update, and polish them to fit your purpose of the moment. Many famous speakers, past and present, have done just that. It is one of the main reasons why it is often so hard to pin down a quotation definitely to an original source. While putting together this collection I have, time and time again, come across sayings which various sources have attributed to different people. There are bound to be errors and distortions, and many readers will no doubt be irritated by apparent mistakes. I offer them an old Texas saying: "It doesn't matter how much milk you spill as long as you don't lose your cow".

I have followed an old journalistic rule; if in doubt, leave out. You will find, therefore, that many of the quotations are not attributed. Next to Shakespeare, the most prolific author of quotes was Anon. You will see his name in most reference books, for a simple reason. *Someone* must have said it first, but if one can't establish the original source it is safer to settle for "Anonymous". I have dispensed even with that overworked device.

The best humour is immediate - extracted from the surroundings and the people present, or from some item in the news. I always keep a close eye on the media and jot down anything which strikes me as absurd and worthy

Introduction

of comment. But one should never use jokes heard recently on television or radio, or stories that are currently "doing the rounds". The audience will almost certainly have heard them too.

I tend to agree with Christian Bovée, who said that "next to being witty yourself, the best thing is to quote another's wit". One should, however, resist the temptation to pepper a speech with numerous quotes. If you do, people think you are merely showing off. Quotations should always be apt - like jokes, they should fit naturally into the speech. They can be used to strengthen your own opinions or to underline a point. Some are also handy if one is addressing a foreign audience. It is more likely to accept a quip if you are quoting one of their own authors (with proper acknowledgement) or a well-known proverb.

Another reason why one has to be careful in the use of wit is that it can be hurtful. GK Chesterton said that "wit is a sword; it is meant to make people feel the point as well as to see it". Marya Mannes put it another way: "Wit has a deadly aim and it is possible to prick a large pretence with a small pin". There are many times when one feels fully justified in doing so, but there is always a danger that the sword - or pin - will end up in your own back. Everyone claims to have a sense of humour, but most of us find it easier to laugh at others than at ourselves.

As the editor of *Punch* for most of the 1970s I presided over the Table - an English institution that predated the *New Yorker*'s Round Table by many decades. Each week, more than a dozen writers and cartoonists gathered for lunch and a battle of wits. We were friends and none of us

Introduction

minded being subjected to mockery: what counted was that the remark should be funny. I had been the financial editor of *The Guardian* prior to my appointment (which some people thought was a good joke itself) so it took me a while to get accustomed to these antics, but I soon came to enjoy them. I was no match for humorists like Alan Coren, Miles Kington, Basil Boothroyd, and Keith Waterhouse but I sometimes managed to score and was delighted to get a laugh. Alas, no-one bothered to keep a record of any of the *bons mots*. Some later turned up in articles for the magazine, but there was no Boswell eagerly writing down everything that was said.

When I left *Punch* to start my own publishing company I found that such foolery was much less welcome in the outside world - people I did business with were often quick to take offence. But at least I had learned to laugh at myself.

Any collection of quotes is bound to reflect the sense of humour of the person who compiled it, and this one is no exception. I am well aware that all humour is subjective: what one man or woman finds funny is liable to leave another stony-faced. I hope, however, that many of the quotations will give you as much pleasure as they have given me and that they will prove to be helpful and inspirational. My thanks are due to Caroline Cook, a long-time colleague and friend, for her assistance and to British Airways for making it possible to publish the *Business Life Book of Wit & Wisdom*.

William Davis

ACCOUNTANTS

Accountants invented actuaries so that they could laugh at someone else.

An auditor is an accountant who comes on the field after the battle is won and bayonets the wounded.

Three men apply for a job as an accountant. They are asked one question: What is two times two? The first two fellows get it right. The third one replies: "What figure did you have in mind, sir?" He gets the job.

An actuary is someone who cannot stand the excitement of chartered accountancy.

An accountant is a man hired to explain that you didn't make the money you did.

ACHIEVEMENT

To accomplish great things we must live as if we were never going to die.

You can get almost anything accomplished if you don't care who gets the credit.

Ned Hay

The surest way to get a thing done is to give it to the busiest man you know, and he'll have his secretary do it.

We can continue to achieve if we don't get too comfortable.

The world is not interested in the storms you encountered, but did you bring in the ship.

It is not enough to aim, you must hit.

Italian proverb

It is not the mountain we conquer but ourselves

Sir Edmund Hillary

ACTION

Man who waits for roast duck to fly into mouth must wait for a very, very long time.

Chinese proverb

Hoping won't make something happen.

Actions speak louder than words - but not as often.

I wondered why somebody didn't do something; then I realised that I was somebody.

You can't build a reputation on what you are going to do.

Henry Ford

Action is eloquence.

If there is no wind, row.

If your ship doesn't come in, swim out to it.

It is better to light a candle than to curse the darkness.

Confucius

Well done is better than well said.

Benjamin Franklin

The actions of men are the best interpreters of their thoughts.

John Locke

There are really only three types of people: those who make things happen, those who watch things happen, and those who say: what happened?

Ann Landers

Never mistake motion for action.

Ernest Hemingway

I want to see you shoot the way you shout.

Theodore Roosevelt

People who know how to act are never preachers.

Ralph Waldo Emerson

Action springs not from thought, but from a readiness for responsibility.

Action will remove the doubt that theory cannot solve.

Chinese proverb

Thunder is good, thunder is impressive; but it is the lightning that does the work.

Mark Twain

ADVERSITY

Adversity reveals genius; prosperity conceals it.

Trouble is only opportunity in work clothes.

Adversity introduces a man to himself.

There is no education like adversity.

When it is dark enough, men see the stars.

In prosperity our friends know us; in adversity we know our friends.

The very difficulty of a problem evokes abilities or talents which would otherwise, in happy times, never emerge to shine.

Horace

Every adversity carries with it the seeds of a greater benefit.

By trying we can easily learn to endure adversity. Another man's, I mean.

Mark Twain

Adversity has the same effect on a man that severe training has on the pugilist - it reduces him to his fighting weight.

Josh Billings

Advise and counsel him. If he does not listen, let adversity teach him.

Japanese proverb

Every calamity is a spur and valuable hint.

Ralph Waldo Emerson

That which does not kill me makes me stronger.

Nietzsche

Learn to see in another's calamity the ills which you should avoid.

Publilius Syrus

The worse the passage the more welcome the port.

ADVERTISING

Advertising is the fine art of convincing people that debt is better than frustration.

In our factory, we make lipstick. In our advertising, we sell hope.

Charles Revlon

The philosophy behind much advertising is based on the old observation that every man is really two men - the man he is and the man he wants to be.

William Feather

Doing business without advertising is like winking at a girl in the dark. You know what you are doing but nobody else does.

I know half the money I spend on advertising is wasted, but I can never find out which half.

John Wanamaker

Advertising is salesmanship in print.

Don't advertise; tell it to a gossip.

A clothing tycoon, Max Hart, summoned his advertising manager to complain about the latest campaign. "Nobody reads that much copy", he asserted. The ad manager begged to differ. "I'll bet you ten dollars, Mr Hart, that I can write a whole newspaper page of solid type and you will read every word of it". The tycoon accepted the bet. "I won't have to write even a paragraph to prove my point", the ad man continued. "I'll just give you the heading: THIS PAGE IS ALL ABOUT MAX HART."

The codfish lays ten thousand eggs,
the homely hen lays one.
The codfish never cackles
to tell you what she's done.
And so we scorn the codfish,
while the humble hen we prize,
Which only goes to show you
that it pays to advertise.

Advertising is like learning - a little is a dangerous thing.

PT Barnum

Promise, large promise, is the soul of an advertisement.

Samuel Johnson

You can fool all of the people all of the time if the advertising is right and the budget is big enough.

Joseph E Levine

The guy you've really got to reach with your advertising is the copywriter for your chief rival's advertising agency. If you can terrorise him, you've got it licked.

Howard L Gossage

Nothing except the Mint can make money without advertising.

Macaulay

When the client moans and sighs
Make his logo twice the size
If he still should prove refractory
Show a picture of his factory
Only in the gravest cases
Should you show the client's faces.

An advertising man dies, and finds himself at the Pearly Gates. St Peter explains that they have a special routine these days for his sort, who have to spend a day in Heaven and one in Hell and choose which they prefer. The ad man's day in Heaven is alright, lying around on clouds playing harps, but a bit boring, really. The next day, in mortal terror, he gets into the lift and is whisked down to Hell.
And walks out onto a golf course, on a beautiful spring day. All his old friends are there, and they have a couple of rounds and then retire to a well-stocked clubhouse. Even the Devil turns out to be a fine chap.
The next day he cheerfully elects for Hell. Down in the lift, and out into scenes of torment and terror this time. Eternal flames, racks, boiling lakes. And the

Devil, grinning in the middle of it all. "Where's the golf, where's the clubhouse?" he asks as he is dragged off. "You don't understand", says the Devil. "Yesterday you were a prospect. Today you're a client."

Echo men are very important in advertising. They are men who follow in the wake of the big executive and echo his sentiments as they are expressed.

Fred Allen

ADVICE

Advice is seldom welcome. Those who need it most like it least.

Samuel Johnson

Socrates was a Greek philosopher who went around giving people good advice. They poisoned him.

I am glad that I paid so little attention to good advice; had I abided by it I might have been saved from some of my most valuable mistakes.

Gene Fowler

To ask advice is nine times out of ten to tout for flattery.

Churton Collins

We ask advice, but we mean approbation.

How we admire the wisdom of those who come to us for good advice!

Advice is information given by someone who can't use it to someone who won't.

Advice is what a person asks for when he wants you to agree with him.

An old man gives good advice to console himself for no longer being able to set a bad example.

Josh Billings

Never trust the advice of a man in difficulties.

When we ask for advice we are usually looking for an accomplice.

He who builds to every man's advice will have a crooked house.

Danish proverb

Nothing is given so freely as advice.

French proverb

No enemy is worse than bad advice.

We may give advice, but we cannot inspire conduct.

You will always find some Eskimos ready to instruct the Congolese on how to cope with heat waves.

Stanislaw Lec

AGE

Strategies are okayed in boardrooms that even a child would say are bound to fail. The problem is, there is never a child in the boardroom.

The young do not know enough to be prudent, and therefore they attempt the impossible, and achieve it, generation after generation.

Pearl S Buck

I'm not young enough to know everything

JM Barrie

You are old when you do more and more for the last time and less and less for the first time.

I will never be an old man. To me, old age is always fifteen years older than I am.

Bernard Baruch

Don't laugh at a youth for his affectations; he is only trying on one face after another to find a face of his own.

Logan Pearsall Smith

A youth without fire is followed by old age without experience.

Charles Colton

The aged love what is practical, while impetuous youth longs only for what is dazzling.

Many a man that can't direct you to a corner drugstore will get a respectful hearing when age has further impaired his mind.

Men of age object too much, consult too long, adventure too little, repent too soon.

Francis Bacon

MIDDLE AGE IS:

When you are warned to slow down by a doctor instead of a policeman.

When you begin to feel on Saturday night the way you used to feel on Monday morning.

When you'd rather pay the piper than dance.

When all you exercise is caution.

When you go out and wind up all in.

When you are impressed not with the fact that the grass is greener on the other side of the fence but rather how difficult the fence looks to get over.

When we can do just as much as ever - but would rather not.

How foolish to think that one can ever slam the door in the face of age. Much wiser to be polite and gracious and ask him to lunch in advance.

Noël Coward

There's one more terrifying fact about old people: I'm going to be one soon.

PJ O'Rourke

Growing old is like being increasingly penalised for a crime you haven't committed.

Anthony Powell

I have my eighty-seventh birthday coming up and people ask what I'd most appreciate getting. I'll tell you: a paternity suit.

George Burns

AMERICA AND AMERICANS

America is so vast that almost everything said about it is likely to be true, and the opposite is probably equally true.

James T Farrell

Americans like fat books and thin women.

Russell Baker

Losing is the great American sin.

John Tunis

.....as American as English muffins and French toast.

When American life is most American it is apt to be most theatrical.

Ralph Waldo Emerson

If American men are obsessed with money, American women are obsessed with weight. The men talk of gain, the women talk of loss, and I do not know which talk is the more boring.

Marya Mannes

The pursuit of happiness, which American citizens are obliged to undertake, tends to involve them in trying to perpetuate the moods, tastes, and aptitudes of youth.

Malcolm Muggeridge

Frustrate a Frenchman, he will drink himself to death; an Irishman, he will die of angry hypertension; a Dane, he will shoot himself; an American, he will get drunk, shoot you, then establish a million-dollar aid programme for your relatives. Then he will die of an ulcer.

Stanley Rudin

Americans are like a rich father who wishes he knew how to give his son the hardships that made him rich.

Robert Frost

America: a land of untold wealth.

Internal Revenue Service

American enterprise: the art of making toeless shoes a fashion rather than a calamity.

America is a vast conspiracy to make you happy.

John Updike

Americans adore me and will go on adoring me until I say something nice about them.

George Bernard Shaw

So much of learning to be an American is learning not to let your individuality become a nuisance.

Edgar Friedenberg

The typical successful American businessman was born in the country, where he worked like hell so he could live in the city, where he worked like hell so he could live in the country.

Don Marquis

Americans hardly ever retire from business; they are either carried out feet first or they jump from a window.

AL Goodheart

ANGER

Never answer a letter while you are angry.

Chinese proverb

Beware the fury of a patient man.

John Dryden

Never forget what a man says to you when he is angry.

Anger is a bad counsellor.

French proverb

The greatest remedy for anger is delay.

Seneca

An angry man is again angry with himself when he returns to reason.

He is a fool who cannot be angry; but he is a wise man who will not.

English proverb

Anger punishes itself.

Growl all day and you'll feel dog tired at night.

A man is as big as the things that annoy him.

Anger makes me mad.

He never let the sun go down on his wrath, though there were some colourful sunsets while it lasted.

AA Thomson (of WG Grace)

A man in a passion rides a horse that runs away with him.

Thomas Fuller

Anger without power is folly.

German proverb

The bare recollection of anger kindles anger.

ANXIETY

Anxiety is a thin stream of fear trickling through the mind. If encouraged, it cuts a channel into which all other thoughts are drained.

The thinner the ice, the more anxious is everyone to see whether it will bear.

Josh Billings

I have a new philosophy. I'm only going to dread one day at a time.

Charles Schulz (Peanuts cartoon)

How much pain have cost us the evils which have never happened!

Thomas Jefferson

As a rule, what is out of sight disturbs men's minds more seriously than what they see.

Julius Caesar

We are often more frightened than hurt; our troubles spring more often from fancy than from reality.

ARGUMENT

You have not converted a man because you have silenced him.

A man never tells you anything until you contradict him.

There is nothing so annoying as arguing with somebody who knows what he is talking about.

If you win all your arguments, you'll end up with no friends.

Silence is one of the hardest things to refute.

A long dispute means both parties are wrong.

Voltaire

I learned long ago never to wrestle with a pig. You get dirty and besides, the pig likes it.

Cyrus Ching

He said true things, but called them by the wrong names.

Robert Browning

I dislike arguments of any kind. They are always vulgar, and often convincing.

Oscar Wilde

What's the use of wasting dynamite when insect powder will do?

The art of being wise is the art of knowing what to overlook.

My sad conviction is that people can only agree about what they're not really interested in.

Bertrand Russell

There is no arguing with Johnson; for when his pistol misses fire, he knocks you down with the butt of it.

Oliver Goldsmith

I like talking to a brick wall; it's the only thing in the world that never contradicts me.

Oscar Wilde

Those who in quarrels interpose,
must often wipe a bloody nose.

John Gay

The only way to get the best of an argument is to avoid it.

Dale Carnegie

When an argument is over, how many weighty reasons does a man recollect which his heat and violence made him utterly forget?

Eustace Budgell

The aim of argument, or of discussion, should not be victory but progress.

Joseph Joubert

Arguments only confirm people in their own opinions.

ATTITUDE

Whenever you are asked if you can do a job, tell them, Certainly I can! - and get busy and find out how to do it.

Theodore Roosevelt

We lost because we told ourselves we lost.

Leo Tolstoy

So long as a man imagines he cannot do this or that, so long is he determined not to do it; and consequently, so long it is impossible to him that he should do it.

Spinoza

Act like a lamb and the wolves will eat you.

Blowing out the other fellow's candle won't make yours shine any brighter.

Your attitude, not your aptitude, will determine your altitude.

I was going to buy a copy of *The Power of Positive Thinking* and then I thought: "What the hell good would that do?"

Ronald Shakes

BANKS

Banking establishments are more dangerous than standing armies.
Jefferson

If you owe a bank enough money you own it.

A banker is a guy who charges you high interest to borrow somebody else's money.

A banker is a man who lends you an umbrella when the weather is fair, and takes it away from you when it rains.
Mark Twain

If money doesn't grow on trees, how come banks continue to sprout branches?

BARGAIN

These days anything you can buy for only twice what it's worth.

Something you cannot use at a price you cannot resist.

Something so reasonably priced that they won't take it back when you find out what's wrong with it.

Necessity never made a good bargain.

A deal in which each party thinks he's cheating the other.

Sometimes one pays most for the things one gets for nothing.
Albert Einstein

BEGINNING

Well begun is half done.
Horace

If we wait for the moment when everything, absolutely everything is ready, we shall never begin.

Ivan Turgenev

I start where the last man left off.

Thomas Edison

He who begins many things finishes but few.

Italian proverb

Nothing is more expensive than a start.

Nietzsche

Everything is difficult at first.

Chinese proverb

The creation of a thousand forests is in one acorn.

Ralph Waldo Emerson

A good beginning makes a good ending.

English proverb

BILLS

Happiness is getting a bill you've already paid, so you can sit down and write a nasty letter.

Some people pay their bills when due, some when overdue, and some never do.

It is only by not paying one's bills that one can hope to live in the memory of the commercial classes.

Oscar Wilde

He that pays last never pays twice.

English proverb

BORES

A yawn is nature's way of giving the person listening to a bore the opportunity to open his mouth.

Somebody's boring me - I think it's me.

Dylan Thomas

A bore is a man who deprives you of solitude without providing you with company.

A healthy male adult bore consumes, each year, one and a half times his own weight in other people's patience.

John Updike

I am one of those unhappy persons who inspire bores to the highest flights of art.

Edith Sitwell

A bore is a man who, when you ask him how he is, he tells you.

Bore: a person who talks when you wish him to listen.

Each man reserves to himself alone the right of being tedious.

Ralph Waldo Emerson

It is the peculiarity of the bore that he is the last person to find himself out.

Oliver Wendell Holmes

BOSS

Some people think Davis has a God complex, but this is absurd. On the seventh day *he* works.

(Of Sammy Davis Jnr)

You can't help liking the managing director - if you don't he fires you.

Whenever you're sitting across from some important person, always picture him there in a suit of long red underwear. That's the way I always operated in business.

Joseph P Kennedy

When I take a long time,
I am slow.
When my boss takes a long time,
he is thorough.
When I don't do it,
I am lazy.
When my boss doesn't do it,
he is too busy.
When I do something without being told,
I am trying to be smart.
When my boss does the same,
that is initiative.
When I please my boss,
I am apple-polishing.
When my boss pleases his boss,
he's co-operating.
When I do good, my boss never remembers.
When I do wrong, he never forgets.

The eye of the master will do more work than both his hands.

Benjamin Franklin

At too many companies, the boss shoots the arrow of managerial performance and then hastily paints the bull's-eye around the spot where it lands.

Warren Buffett

Boss: One who's late when you're early and early when you're late.

BRIBERY AND CORRUPTION

A silver key can open an iron lock.

English saying

A friend that you buy with presents will be bought from you.

Thomas Fuller

The jingle of the guinea helps the hurt that honour feels.

Tennyson

A dog will not howl if you beat him with a bone.
Proverb

He refuseth the bribe but putteth forth his hand.
English proverb

A conscience which has been bought once will be bought twice.

Public money is like holy water; everyone helps himself to it.
Italian proverb

I just received the following wire from my generous Daddy: "Dear Jack, don't buy a single vote more than necessary. I'll be damned if I'm going to pay for a landslide".
John F Kennedy

Every man has his price.
Sir Robert Walpole

BUDGET

Merely a mathematical confirmation of your suspicions.

A budget is a formula for telling you that you need a raise.

A budget is a sort of conscience which doesn't keep you from spending, but makes you feel guilty about it.

Budgeting: a method of worrying before you spend instead of afterward.

A device to tell you where your money should have gone.

The trouble with the average family budget is that at the end of the money there's too much month left.

Some people go over their budgets very carefully every month, others just go over them.

A minister of finance is a legally authorised pickpocket.

Paul Ramadier

BUREAUCRACY

Bureaucrats write memoranda both because they appear to be busy when they are writing and because the memos, once written, immediately become proof that they were busy.

Charles Peters

The only thing that saves us from bureaucracy is its inefficiency.

Eugene McCarthy

The longer the title, the less important the job.

A civil servant doesn't make jokes.

Eugène Ionesco

There is something about a bureaucrat that does not like a poem.

Gore Vidal

Bureaucracy is a giant mechanism operated by pygmies.

Balzac

Bureaucracy is the layer, or layers, of management that lies between the person who has decision-making authority on a project and the highest-level person who is working on it full-time.

Herbert Rees

The perfect bureaucrat everywhere is the man who manages to make no decisions and escape all responsibility.

Brooks Atkinson

CARS

It's not a cheaper car that people want. It's an expensive car that costs less.

These are difficult days for car manufacturers: they're thinking up ways to make their products safer and new names to make them sound more dangerous.

People on horses look better than they are. People in cars look worse than they are.

Marya Mannes

There are no liberals behind steering wheels.

Russell Baker

A pedestrian is a man who has two cars - one being driven by his wife, the other by one of his children.

Robert Bradbury

No other man-made device since the shields and lances of the ancient knights fulfils a man's ego like an automobile.

Lord Rootes

Car: a convenient place to sit out a traffic jam.

Classic car: a car so old, it's paid for.

The more parking spaces you provide, the more cars will come to fill them. It is like feeding pigeons.

Sir Hugh Casson

CHANGE

You cannot become what you want to be by remaining what you are.

The one unchangeable certainty is that nothing is unchangeable or certain.

John F Kennedy

It is not the strongest of the species that survive nor the most intelligent, but the ones most responsive to change.

Charles Darwin

The art of progress is to preserve order amid change and to preserve change amid order.

Progress is impossible without change; and those who cannot change their minds cannot change anything.

George Bernard Shaw

There is no way to make people like change. You can only make them feel less threatened by it.

There is nothing permanent except change.

Greek proverb

To remain young one must change.

Never leave well-enough alone.

It is the nature of a man as he grows older to protest against change, particularly change for the better.

John Steinbeck

COMMITMENT

People must believe that a task is inherently worthwhile if they are to be committed to it.

What is the difference between a contribution to a cause and a total commitment? It's like bacon and egg - the chicken has made a contribution, but the pig is totally committed.

Consider the postage stamp. Its usefulness consists in the ability to stick to one thing till it gets there.

COMMITTEES

A committee is a group of people who keep minutes and waste hours.

A committee is a collection of the unfit chosen from the unwilling by the incompetent to do the necessary.

A committee is a *cul-de-sac* to which ideas are lured and then quietly strangled.

Nothing is ever accomplished by a committee unless it consists of three members, one of which happens to be sick and another absent.

COMMON SENSE

Common sense is not so common.

French proverb

Common sense is instinct, and enough of it is genius.

Common sense is in spite of, not the result of, education.

Horace Greeley

Fine sense and exalted sense are not half so useful as common sense.

Alexander Pope

There is nobody so irritating as somebody with less intelligence and more sense than we have.

Don Herold

COMMUNICATION

The single biggest problem in communication is the illusion that it has taken place.

George Bernard Shaw

If you don't give people information, they'll make up something to fill the void.

Carla O'Dell

It is difficult to get a man to understand something when his salary depends upon his not understanding it.

Upton Sinclair

Kindly inform troops immediately that all communications have broken down.

Ashleigh Brilliant

The communicator is the person who can make himself clear to himself first.

Paul Griffith

Half the world is composed of people who have something to say and can't, and the other half who have nothing to say and keep on saying it.

Robert Frost

If people around you will not hear you, fall down before them and beg their forgiveness, for in truth you are to blame.

Dostoevsky

The most important thing in communication is to hear what isn't being said.

Peter Drucker

It ain't watcha say, it's the way howcha say it.

Louis Armstrong

You can stroke people with words.

F Scott Fitzgerald

The best way to nourish the grass roots is with bullshit.

When the eyes say one thing and the tongue another, a practised man relies on the language of the first.

Ralph Waldo Emerson

Words are, of course, the most powerful drug used by mankind.

Rudyard Kipling

A trembling hand, like a clenched fist, can speak volumes.

When ideas fail, words come in very handy.

Goethe

I told the traffic warden to go forth and multiply, though not exactly in those words.

Woody Allen

A good head and good heart are always a formidable combination. But when you add to that a literate tongue or pen, then you have something very special.

Nelson Mandela

COMPETITION

If you can't win, make the fellow ahead of you break the record.

The competitor to be feared is one who never bothers about you at all, but goes on making his own business better all the time.

Henry Ford

Every morning in Africa, a gazelle wakes up. It knows it must outrun the fastest lion or it will be killed. Every morning in Africa, a lion wakes up. It knows it must run faster than the slowest gazelle, or it will starve. It doesn't matter whether you are a lion or a gazelle - when the sun comes up, you'd better be running.

African proverb

We throw all our attention on the utterly idle question whether A has done as well as B, when the only question is whether A has done as well as he could.

A horse never runs so fast as when he has other horses to catch up and outpace.

Those who will only compete when they can dominate are not actually competing at all.
Thomas Paulman

COMPROMISE

It is better to lose the saddle than the horse.
Italian proverb

A lean compromise is better than a fat lawsuit.

Lots of times you have to pretend to join a parade in which you are not really interested, in order to get where you're going.
Christopher Morley

One of the most important trips a man can make is that involved in meeting the other fellow halfway.

Better bend than break.
Scottish proverb

A compromise is the art of dividing a cake in such a way that everyone believes that he has got the biggest piece.
Former German Chancellor Ludwig Erhard

COMPUTERS

Computers will never replace man entirely until they learn to laugh at the boss's jokes.

The real danger is not that computers will begin to think like men, but that men will begin to think like computers.

A computer can do more work faster than a human because it doesn't have to answer the phone.

We seem to be approaching an advanced state in human progress where people are perfect and anything that's wrong is the fault of computers.

Computers are definitely smarter than people. When have you ever heard of six computers getting together to form a committee?

Computers are useless. They can only give you answers.

Pablo Picasso

To err is human but to really foul up requires a computer.

CONFORMITY

Conformity is the jailer of freedom and the enemy of growth.

John F Kennedy

The great majority of men grow up and grow old in seeming and following.

Ralph Waldo Emerson

Conventional people are roused to fury by departure from convention, largely because they regard such departure as criticism of themselves.

Bertrand Russell

Oh let us love our occupations,
Bless the squire and his relations,
Live upon our daily rations,
And always know our proper stations.

Charles Dickens

Success, recognition, and conformity are the bywords of the modern world where everyone seems to crave the anesthetizing security of being identified with the majority.

Martin Luther King Jr

No one can possibly achieve any real and lasting success or get rich in business by being a conformist.

J Paul Getty

CONSULTANTS

A consultant is someone whose approval is sought after a decision has been made.

After the ship has sunk, a consultant knows how it might have been saved.

Consultant: an expert called in when nobody wants to take the blame for what is going wrong.

A consultant is someone who saves his client almost enough to pay his fee.

If it ain't broke, don't fix it - unless you are a consultant.

COURAGE

Fear that has said its prayers.

No one can answer for his courage when he has never been in danger.

Courage is often just ignorance of the facts.

Let me win, but if I cannot win, let me be brave in the attempt.

Special Olympics motto

It is easy to be brave from a safe distance.

Always do what you are
afraid to do.
Ralph Waldo Emerson

When the mouse laughs at
the cat, there is a hole
nearby.
Nigerian proverb

Audacity augments
courage; hesitation, fear.

"I'm very brave generally",
he went on in a low voice:
"only today I happen to
have a headache."
Lewis Carroll

It is better to err on the side
of daring than on the side of
caution.
Alvin Toffler

Success is not final; failure
is not fatal; it is the courage
to continue that counts.
Winston Churchill

COURTESY

A form of polite behaviour
practised by civilised
people when they have
time.

Good manners are made up
of petty sacrifices.

All doors open to courtesy.

Good breeding consists in
concealing how much we
think of ourselves and how
little we think of the other
person.
Mark Twain

Politeness: the most
acceptable hypocrisy.
Ambrose Bierce

The lie is the basic building
block of good manners.

The test of good manners is
to be patient with bad ones.

Manners make the fortune of the ambitious youth.
Ralph Waldo Emerson

The real proof of courtesy is to have the same ailment as the other person is describing and not to mention it.

We cannot always oblige, but we can always speak obligingly.
Voltaire

Etiquette: learning to yawn with your mouth closed.

CRIME

A criminal is a person with predatory instincts who has not sufficient capital to form a corporation.
Howard Scott

The only way to make sure that crime doesn't pay is to have the government take it over and run it.

I was going to read the report about the rising crime rate - but somebody stole it.

A kleptomaniac is a person who helps himself because he can't help himself.

We enact many laws that manufacture criminals, and then a few that punish them.

We don't seem to be able to check crime, so why not legalise it and then tax it out of business.
Will Rogers

Whoever profits by the crime is guilty of it.
French proverb

He who holds the ladder is as bad as the thief.
German proverb

Most men only commit great crimes because of their scruples about petty ones.

Cardinal de Retz

Opportunity makes the thief.

English proverb

It was beautiful and simple as all truly great swindles are.

O Henry

CRITICISM

Don't find fault; find a remedy.

Henry Ford

A successful man is one who can lay a firm foundation with the bricks that others throw at him.

David Brinkley

To avoid criticism, do nothing, say nothing, be nothing.

Elbert Hubbard

A critic is a man who knows the way but can't drive the car.

Kenneth Tynan

Critics are like eunuchs in a harem: they know how it's done, they've seen it done every day, but they're unable to do it themselves.

Brendan Behan

Taking to pieces is the trade of those who cannot construct.

Ralph Waldo Emerson

Criticism should be like a sandwich. If you want to motivate people, slip the criticism in between layers of praise.

A critic is a legless man who teaches running.

Channing Pollock

They who are to be judges must also be performers.

Aristotle

Criticism comes easier than craftsmanship.

Silence is sometimes the severest criticism.
Charles Buxton

Even the lion has to defend himself against flies.
German proverb

How much better the world would be if we let opportunity do all the knocking.

Critics are like brushers of other men's clothes.
English saying

If you stop every time a dog barks, your road will never end.

Arab proverb

CUSTOMERS

Consumers are statistics. Customers are people.

It is not the employer who pays the wages. Employers only handle money. It is the customer who pays the wages.

Henry Ford

A grocery clerk, tired of his job, quit to become a traffic policeman. After a few days, a friend asked him how he liked his new job. He said: "The pay and hours aren't too good, but at least the customer is always wrong".

You can automate the production of cars but you cannot automate the production of customers.
Henry Ford

About the only people who don't get customers coming back complaining are parachute manufacturers.

When you are skinning your customers, you should leave some skin on to grow so that you can skin them again.

Nikita Khrushchev

CYNIC

A cynic is not merely one who reads bitter lessons from the past; he is one who is prematurely disappointed in the future.

Sydney Harris

What is a cynic? A man who knows the price of everything and the value of nothing.

Oscar Wilde

A cynic is just a man who found out when he was about ten that there wasn't any Santa Claus, and he's still upset.

James Cozzens

Cynics are only happy in making the world as barren for others as they have made it for themselves.

George Meredith

Cynic: a blackguard whose faulty vision sees things as they are, not as they ought to be.

Ambrose Bierce

Cynic: a sentimentalist on guard.

No man in his heart is quite so cynical as a well-bred woman.

Somerset Maugham

DEBT

Running into debt isn't such a bad thing. It's running into your creditors that's so embarrassing.

It is hard to pay for bread that has been eaten.

Danish proverb

The borrower is servant to the lender.

Bible

An acquaintance is a person we know well enough to borrow from but not well enough to lend to.

Ambrose Bierce

Live within your income even if you have to borrow to do it.

Josh Billings

Out of debt, out of danger.

Creditors have better memories than debtors.

English proverb

Debts and lies are generally mixed together.

Rabelais

When some men discharge an obligation you can hear the report for miles around.

Mark Twain

The moment you make a man feel the weight of an obligation, he will become your enemy.

One must have some sort of occupation nowadays. If I hadn't my debts I shouldn't have anything to think about.

Oscar Wilde

DELEGATION

Don't do anything someone else can do for you.

Executive ability is deciding quickly and getting someone else to do the work.

When you do for a man what he can and should do for himself, you do him a great disservice.

Benjamin Franklin

A real executive goes around with a worried look on his assistants' faces.

Vince Lombardi

Guidelines for Bureaucrats:
1. When in charge, ponder.
2. When in trouble, delegate.
3. When in doubt, mumble.

Don't tell people how to do things. Tell them what to do and let them surprise you with their results.

George S Patton

Here lies a man who knew how to enlist the service of better men than himself.

Tombstone of Andrew Carnegie

DIGNITY

One thing that cannot be preserved in alcohol.

The eagle does not catch flies.

It is easier to grow in dignity than to make a start.

I know of no case where a man added to his dignity by standing on it.

Winston Churchill

Only man can be absurd, for only man can be dignified.

GK Chesterton

The only kind of dignity which is genuine is that which is not diminished by the indifference of others.

Dag Hammerskjöld

DISAPPOINTMENT

Disappointments should be cremated, not embalmed.

Too many people miss the silver lining because they're expecting gold.

Maurice Scitter

Disappointment should always be taken as a stimulant, and never viewed as a discouragement.

Blessed is he who expects nothing, for he shall never be disappointed.

Pope

Nothing is as good as it seems beforehand.

George Eliot

Disappointment is the nurse of wisdom.

DISCRETION

I have never been hurt by anything I didn't say.

Calvin Coolidge

When shut out of the room, you must not peep through the keyhole. Either break down the door or go away.

Dag Hammarskjöld

What is called discretion in men is called cunning in animals.

Jean de la Fontaine

A wise man sees as much as he ought, not as much as he can.

Montaigne

It is not good to wake a sleeping lion.

There's a time to wink as well as to see.

Benjamin Franklin

The better part of valour is discretion.

Shakespeare

Great ability without discretion comes almost invariably to a tragic end.

Gambetta

DOUBT

Who knows nothing doubts nothing.

French proverb

To believe with certainty we must begin with doubting.

Stanislaw I, King of Poland

Doubt makes the mountain which faith can move.

When in doubt, tell the truth.

Mark Twain

Galileo called doubt the father of invention: it is certainly the pioneer.

Bovée

I love to doubt as well as know.

Dante

Our doubts are traitors and make us lose the good we oft might win, by fearing to attempt.

Shakespeare

The only limit to our realisation of tomorrow will be our doubts of today.

Franklin D Roosevelt

Doubt and mistrust are the mere panic of timid imagination, which the steadfast heart will conquer, and the large mind transcend.

Helen Keller

DREAMS

Some men see things as they are and ask why. I dream things that never were and say, why not?

George Bernard Shaw

All men of action are dreamers.

If you can dream it, you can do it.

Walt Disney

To make your dream come true, you have to stay awake.

Everything starts as somebody's daydream.

Dreams come true; without that possibility, nature would not incite us to have them.

John Updike

Dreamers exist to keep the dreams alive until the non-dreamers are ready to dream.

Pierre LeClerc

If you have built castles in the air, your work need not be lost; that is where they should be. Now put the foundations under them.

Henry Thoreau

DRESS

It is an interesting question how far men would retain their relative rank if they were divested of their clothes.

Henry Thoreau

Good clothes open all doors.

No fine clothes can hide the clown.

A well-tied tie is the first serious step in life.

Oscar Wilde

By the husk you may guess at the nut.

Thomas Fuller

The first thing the first couple did after committing the first sin was to get dressed. Thus Adam and Eve started the world of fashion, and styles have been changing ever since.

Women's clothes: never wear anything that panics the cat.

PJ O'Rourke

There'll be little change in men's pockets this year.

You should never have your best trousers on when you go out to fight for freedom and truth.

Henrik Ibsen

If Botticelli were alive today he'd be working for *Vogue*.

Peter Ustinov

DRINK

What the sober man thinks the drunkard tells.

One of the disadvantages of wine is that it makes a man mistake words for thoughts.

Samuel Johnson

Don't make your nose blush for the sins of your mouth.

He drank like a fish, if drinking nothing but water could be so described.

I've formed a new organisation called Alcoholics Unanimous. If you don't feel like a drink, you ring another member and he comes over to persuade you.

Richard Harris

An honest man that is not quite sober has nothing to fear.

I am speaking to you tonight under a severe handicap. I'm sober.

I must get out of these wet clothes and into a dry martini.

Alexander Woollcott

Friendships are not always preserved in alcohol.

There is a devil in every berry of the grape.

Koran

It (drink) provokes the desire, but takes away the performance.

Shakespeare

Alcoholic: someone you don't like who drinks as much as you do.

Dylan Thomas

Never drink on an empty wallet.

I always keep a stimulant handy in case I see a snake - which I also keep handy.

WC Fields

My dad was the town drunk. A lot of times that's not so bad - but New York City?

Henny Youngman

Actually, it only takes one drink to get me loaded. Trouble is, I can't remember if it's the thirteenth or fourteenth.

George Burns

I know I'm drinking myself to a slow death, but I'm in no hurry.

Robert Benchley

"I think this calls for a drink" has long been one of our national slogans.

James Thurber

He often sits up late working on a case of Scotch.

The bartender looked up and saw a pink elephant, a green cat and a yellow snake at the bar. "You're a little early, boys", he said. "He hasn't come in yet."

The bubble winked at me and said, "You'll miss me, brother, when you're dead".

Oliver Herford on champagne

Better to pay the tavernkeeper than the druggist.

Any port in a storm.

Wine improves with age - I
like it more the older I get.

Never drink anything
without smelling it, never
sign anything without first
reading it.

Never dive into pools of
depths unknown,
And rarely drink - if you are
alone.

ECONOMICS

The instability of the economy is equalled only by the instability of the economists.

John H Williams

If you're not confused, you're not paying attention.

A man can be forgiven a lot if he can quote Shakespeare in an economic crisis.

Prince Philip

If economists could manage to get themselves thought of as humble, competent people, on a level with dentists, that would be splendid.

John Maynard Keynes

If all economists were laid end to end, they would not reach a conclusion.

George Bernard Shaw

An economist is a man who states the obvious in terms of the incomprehensible.

Making a speech on economics is a bit like pissing down your leg. It seems hot to you but never to anyone else.

Lyndon B Johnson

Trickle-down theory: the less than elegant metaphor that if one feeds the horse enough oats, some will pass through to the road for the sparrows.

JK Galbraith

I think the light at the end of the economic tunnel is starting to flicker again.

It's a recession when your neighbour loses his job, it's a depression when you lose your own.

As I interpret the president, we're now at the end of the beginning of the upturn of the downturn.

John F Kennedy (when Senator)

Economics is like being lost in the woods. How can you tell where you are going if you don't even know where you are?

Take care to be an economist in prosperity; there is no fear of your not being one in adversity.

Business slump: when sales are down 10 per cent and sales meetings are up 100 per cent.

EMPLOYEE RELATIONS

Industrial relations are like sexual relations. They should be between two consenting parties.

You can't shake hands with a clenched fist.

Indira Gandhi

Employees make the best product when they like where they work.

A trade union is an island of anarchy in a sea of chaos.

Aneurin Bevan

Good industrial relations is showing people that they are not just employees but human beings you are interested in.

The latest argument at a works renowned for its management problems got senior executives so upset that they began to stab each other in the front.

You can handle people more successfully by enlisting their feelings than by convincing their reason.

Remember that a man's name is, to him, the sweetest and most important sound in any language.

Dale Carnegie

If you scream at workers, you may not discover the real problem.

ENEMIES

Love your enemies. At least they don't try to borrow money from you.

Speak well of your enemies, Sir, you made them.

Don't think there are no crocodiles because the water is calm.

Malayan proverb

A man cannot be too careful in the choice of his enemies.

Oscar Wilde

He makes no friends who never made a foe.

Tennyson

There is nothing like the sight of an old enemy down on his luck.

Euripides

I never thought myself beaten so long as I could present a front to the enemy. If I was beaten at one point I went to another, and in that way I won all my victories.

Duke of Wellington

Man is his own worst enemy.

Cicero

A man's greatness can be measured by his enemy.

Love your enemies, for they tell you your faults.

Benjamin Franklin

His must be a very wretched fortune who has no enemy.

Latin proverb

Enemies are so stimulating.

Katherine Hepburn

It's easier to forgive an enemy once you've got even with him.

Pay attention to your enemies, for they are the first to discover your mistakes.

A strong foe is better than a weak friend.

There is no safety in regaining the favours of an enemy.

ENTHUSIASM

Nothing is so contagious as enthusiasm.

Samuel Taylor Coleridge

You can do anything if you have enthusiasm. Enthusiasm is the yeast that makes your hopes rise to the stars. With it, there is accomplishment. Without it there are only alibis.

Henry Ford

If you aren't fired with enthusiasm, you will be fired by enthusiasm.

Leadership is leaving zest in your wake.

Tom Peters

One man has enthusiasm for 30 minutes, another for 30 days, but it is the man who has it for 30 years who makes a success of life.

What this country needs is more young people who will carry to their jobs the same enthusiasm for getting ahead that they display in traffic.

We act as though comfort and luxury were the chief requirements of life, when all that we need to make us happy is something to be enthusiastic about.

In things pertaining to enthusiasm, no man is sane who does not know how to be insane on proper occasions.

The worst bankrupt in the world is the man who has lost his enthusiasm.

I prefer the errors of enthusiasm to the indifference of wisdom.

Anatole France

The world belongs to the enthusiast who keeps cool.

ENVY

Envy is the tax which all distinction must pay.

Ralph Waldo Emerson

It is better to be envied than to be pitied.

Herodotus

Let age, not envy, draw wrinkles on thy cheeks.

Sir Thomas Browne

Envy is a kind of praise.

John Gay

The envious die not once, but as oft as the envied win applause.

Even success softens not the heart of the envious.

Pindar

A show of envy is an insult to oneself.

Yevgeny Yevtushenko

As iron is eaten away by rust, so the envious are consumed by their own passion.

Antisthenes

If there is any sin more deadly than envy, it is being pleased at being envied.

Richard Armour

EQUALITY

All men are born equal, but quite a few eventually get over it.

The defect with equality is that we only desire it with our superiors.

Henry Becque

All animals are equal, but some are more equal than others.

George Orwell, *Animal Farm*

The only real equality is in the cemetery.

German proverb

We clamour for equality chiefly in matters in which we ourselves cannot hope to obtain excellence.

Eric Hoffer

The principle of equality does not destroy the imagination, but lowers its flight to the level of the earth.

Alexis de Tocqueville

We are all Adam's children, but silk makes the difference.

Thomas Fuller

EUROPEANS

The French want no-one to be their superior. The English want inferiors.

Alexis de Tocqueville

How can you expect to govern a country that has 246 kinds of cheese?

Charles de Gaulle

The Germans always buy a platform ticket before they storm a railway station.

Nietzsche

When a Swiss banker jumps out of the window, jump after him. There must be money to be made.

Voltaire

An Englishman, even if he is alone, forms an orderly queue of one.

George Mikes

The Irish are a fair people - they never speak well of one another.

Samuel Johnson

It is commonly known that one of the worst things for a Norwegian is to be taken in by a Dane.

Among the Greeks every man is an actor.

Juvenal

A German businessman who had fallen on hard times decided to commit suicide. He went to the roof of a high building but hesitated whether to jump or not. Instead of pleading with him not to give up, as they would have done in Britain, several Germans in the crowd shouted "Jump, you coward". And he did.

Adolph Schalk, The Germans

To be or not to be, that is the question. But the question is badly formulated.

(If Shakespeare had been a Frenchman)

An Englishman's mind works best when it's almost too late.

Lord d'Abernon

Rule Britannia Britannia waives the rules!

I once wrote that in order to reach for the truth the Germans add, the French subtract, and the English change the subject. I did not include the Americans, since they so often give the impression that they already have the truth.

Peter Ustinov

When we're in trouble, we talk. When the Walloons talk, they are in trouble.

Flemish joke

Beware of Greeks bearing gifts? Nonsense! Instead, beware of being unprepared when the gifts are brought.

The English may not like music, but they absolutely love the noise it makes.

Sir Thomas Beecham

It is unthinkable for a Frenchman to arrive at middle age without having syphilis and the Croix de la Légion d'Honneur.

André Gide

Very little counts for less in Italy than the state.

Peter Nichols

It is never difficult to distinguish between a Scotsman with a grievance and a ray of sunshine.

PG Wodehouse

When an Englishman is totally incapable of doing any work whatsoever, he describes himself on his income-tax form as a "gentleman".

Robert Lynd

There are three things to beware of: the hoof of a horse, the horn of a bull, and the smile of an Englishman.

Seamus MacManus

If it was raining soup, the Irish would be out with forks.

Brendan Behan

The British tourist is always happy abroad as long as the natives are waiters.

Robert Morley

A French member of parliament went to sleep for half an hour during a debate and when he woke he found that he had been Prime Minister twice.

Oswald Lewis

Heaven is a French cook, an English policeman, a German engineer, an Italian lover, and everything organised by the Swiss. Hell is an English cook, a French engineer, a German policeman, a Swiss lover, and everything organised by the Italians.

The Irish people do not gladly suffer common sense.

Oliver St John Gogarty

Every St Patrick's Day every Irishman goes out to find another Irishman to make a speech to.

Shane Leslie

EXAMPLE

Example is the greatest of all seducers.

French proverb

Few things are harder to put up with than the annoyance of a good example.

Mark Twain

Example is better than following it.

Ambrose Bierce

People seldom improve when they have no model but themselves to copy after.

Goldsmith

Example is the best precept.

Aesop

EXCELLENCE

Nobody gets to run the mill by doing run-of-the-mill work.

Learn to say "no" to the good so you can say "yes" to the best.

Striving for excellence motivates you; striving for perfection is demoralising.

If you don't do it excellently, don't do it at all. Because if it's not excellent, it won't be profitable or fun, and if you're not in business for fun or profit, what the hell are you doing there?

Robert Townsend

The society which scorns excellence in plumbing, because plumbing is a humble activity, and tolerates shoddiness in philosophy, because it is an exalted activity, will have neither good plumbing nor good philosophy. Neither will hold water.

It takes a long time to bring excellence to maturity.

Either dance well or quit the ballroom.

Greek proverb

Life's like a play: it's not the length, but the excellence of the acting that matters.

Seneca

EXCESS

Excess on occasion is exhilarating. It prevents moderation from acquiring the deadening effect of a habit.

Somerset Maugham

I hate to advocate drugs, alcohol, violence, or insanity to anyone, but they've always worked for me.

Hunter S Thompson

Minds, like bodies, will often fall into a pimpled, ill-conditioned state from mere excess of comfort.

Montaigne

You cannot have everything. I mean where would you put it?

Steven Wright

With all the unrest in the world, I don't think anybody should have a yacht that sleeps more than twelve.

Tony Curtis, Some Like it Hot

It is just as unpleasant to get more than you bargain for as to get less.

George Bernard Shaw

EXCUSES

Justifying a fault doubles it.

Excuses interest no-one except the competition.

Unwillingness easily finds an excuse.

Benjamin Franklin

An excuse is worse and more terrible than a lie; for an excuse is a lie guarded.

Alexander Pope

Several excuses are always less convincing than one.

Aldous Huxley

Bad excuses are worse than none.

Thomas Fuller

One unable to dance blames the unevenness of the floor.

Malay proverb

EXECUTIVE

A man who can take two hours for lunch without hindering production.

A man who talks to visitors while the employees get their work done.

One who never puts off until tomorrow what he can get someone else to do today.

A man who believes in sharing the credit with the man who did the work.

A man who has an infinite capacity for taking planes.

The best executive is the one who has sense enough to pick good men to do what he wants done, and self-restraint enough to keep from meddling with them while they do it.

Theodore Roosevelt

EXPENSES

In Brighton she was
Brenda,
She was Patsy up in Perth,
In Cambridge she was
Candida,
The sweetest girl on earth.
In Stafford she was Stella,
The pick of all the bunch,
But down on his expenses,
She was *Petrol*, *Oil* and
Lunch.

EXPERIENCE

Experience teaches you to recognise a mistake when you have made it again.

When you are young, you are not experienced enough to know you cannot possibly do the things you are doing.

Experience is what happens to you while you are making other plans.

Good judgement comes from experience, and experience - well, that comes from poor judgement.

We learn from experience. A man never wakes up his second baby just to see it smile.

Experience is the name everyone gives to his mistakes.

Oscar Wilde

Experience is the best schoolmaster, only the school fees are heavy.

Carlyle

After the event, even a fool is wise.

Homer

He jests at scars that never felt a wound.

Shakespeare

And others' follies teach us not,
Nor much their wisdom teaches;
And most, of sterling worth, is what
Our own experience preaches.

Tennyson

One thorn of experience is worth a wilderness of warning.

Experience teaches us at the expense of our illusions

Experience is one thing you can't get for nothing.

By the time a man learns to watch his step, he isn't going anywhere.

Experience is what permits you to make the same mistake again without getting caught.

Experience is what keeps a man who makes the same mistake twice from admitting it the third time round.

Experience is a comb which nature gives to men when they are bald.
> **Eastern proverb**

He who has once burnt his mouth always blows his soup.
> **German proverb**

He who has been bitten by a snake fears a piece of string.
> **Persian proverb**

What is experience? A poor little hut constructed from the ruins of the palace of gold and marble called our illusions.
> **Joseph Roux**

EXPERT

An expert is one who knows more and more about less and less.

From "ex", a has-been and "spurt" a drip under pressure.

Make three correct guesses consecutively and you will establish yourself as an expert.
> **Lawrence Peter**

Beware of being marched in bold logic by the priestly up the garden path.

If women do what efficiency experts do, it's called nagging.

Experts should be on tap but never on top.
> **Winston Churchill**

An efficiency expert attended a performance of Schubert's *Unfinished Symphony* and issued the following critique:

1. For most of the performance, the four oboe players had nothing to do. They should be eliminated and their work spread out over the entire orchestra.
2. Forty violins were playing identical notes. This seemed unnecessary, and this section should be drastically cut.
3. The horns repeated the passages already played by the strings. If this duplication was eliminated, the concert could be reduced by twenty minutes.

FAILURE

Show me a thoroughly satisfied man, and I will show you a failure.

Thomas Edison

Failure is a man who has blundered, but is not able to cash in on his experience.

If at first you don't succeed, destroy all evidence that you tried.

Failure is the opportunity to begin again, more intelligently.

Henry Ford

A man fails many times but he isn't a failure until he begins to blame somebody else.

J Paul Getty

There's only one way you can fail, and that's to quit.

Failure is the path of least persistence.

I have had a lot of success with failure.

Thomas Edison

Success covers a multitude of blunders.

George Bernard Shaw

When I was a young man I observed that nine out of ten things I did were failures. I didn't want to be a failure, so I did ten times more work.

George Bernard Shaw

Everyone pushes a falling fence.

Chinese proverb

He who never fails will never grow rich.

Never give a man up until he has failed at something he likes.

There is the greatest practical benefit in making a few failures early in life.

TH Huxley

There is always time for failure.

John Mortimer

Results? Why, man, I've gotten a lot of results. I know 50,000 things that won't work.

Thomas Edison

FAME

What a heavy burden is a name that has become too famous.

Voltaire

Fame usually comes to those who are thinking about something else.

Oliver Wendell Holmes

A celebrity is a person who works hard all his life to become well known, and then wears dark glasses to avoid being recognised.

Fred Allen

The final test of fame is to have a crazy person imagine he is you.

Fame is proof that people are gullible.

Ralph Waldo Emerson

Some are born great, some achieve greatness, and some hire public relations officers.

Popularity? It is glory's small change.

Victor Hugo

Fame is nothing but the sum of all misunderstandings collected around a name.

Rainer Maria Rilke

It took me fifteen years to discover that I had no talent for writing, but I couldn't give it up because by that time I was too famous.

Robert Benchley

Fame is the thirst of youth.
Lord Byron

Fame is a magnifying glass.
English proverb

Fame is a constant effort.

FARMING

Farming is not really a business: it is an occupation.
William E Woodward

A farmer is always going to be rich next year.

A farm is an irregular patch of nettles bound by short-term notes, containing a fool and his wife who didn't know enough to stay in the city.
SJ Perelman

Farming looks mighty easy when your plow is a pencil, and you're a thousand miles from the cornfield.
Dwight D Eisenhower

A farm is a section of land on which if you get up early enough mornings and work late enough nights, you'll make money - if you strike oil.

One good thing about living on a farm is that you can fight with your wife without being heard.
Kim Hubbard

FATE

Whatever limits us, we call Fate.
Ralph Waldo Emerson

Lots of folks confuse bad management with destiny.
Kim Hubbard

Unseen, in the background, Fate was quietly slipping the lead into the boxing glove.
PG Wodehouse

If fate means you to lose, give him a good fight anyhow.

William McFee

Fate leads the willing, and drags along the reluctant.

Seneca

We make our fortunes and we call them fate.

Disraeli

No-one knows what will happen to him before sunset.

Turkish proverb

FAULTS

People who have no faults are terrible; there is no way of taking advantage of them.

Anatole France

The greatest of faults, I should say, is to be conscious of none.

Thomas Carlyle

If we had no faults we should not take so much pleasure in noticing them in others.

La Rochefoucauld

A man without faults is a mountain without crevasses. He is of no interest to me.

René Char

Certain defects are necessary for the existence of individuality.

Goethe

None of us can stand other people having the same faults as ourselves.

Oscar Wilde

We keep deceiving ourselves in regard to our faults, until we at last come to look upon them as virtues.

Heine

He is lifeless that is faultless.

English proverb

FOOD

If you are ever at a loss to support a flagging conversation, introduce the subject of eating.
Leigh Hunt

The lunches of fifty-seven years had caused his chest to slip down into the mezzanine floor.
PG Wodehouse

Asparagus inspires gentle thoughts.
Charles Lamb

We lived for days on nothing but food and water.
WC Fields

Eat drink and be merry, for tomorrow we diet.

Diets are for those who are thick and tired of it.

Minutes at the table don't put on weight - it's the seconds.

The one thing harder than sticking to a diet is keeping quiet about it.

Losing weight is a triumph of mind over platter.

Lunch Hollywood style - a hot dog and vintage wine.
Harry Kurnitz

I just love Chinese food. My favourite dish is number 27.

I could never learn to like her - except on a raft at sea with no other provisions in sight.
Mark Twain

I will not eat oysters. I want my food dead. Not sick, not wounded, dead.
Woody Allen

Beulah, peel me a grape.
Mae West

I am not hungry; but thank goodness I am greedy.
Punch

No-one goes to that restaurant any more - it's too crowded.

The only food that doesn't go up in price is food for thought.

He who indulges, bulges.

When you go to a restaurant, always ask for a table near a waiter.

A gourmet is just a glutton with brains.

Phillip Haberman

The glutton digs his grave with his teeth.

English proverb

FOOLS

A prosperous fool is a grievous burden.

Aeschylus

Most fools think they are only ignorant.

Benjamin Franklin

A fool always finds one still more foolish to admire him.

Nothing is more humiliating than to see idiots succeed in enterprises we have failed in.

Gustave Flaubert

A fool and his money are soon parted.

English proverb

The most artful part in a play is the fool's.

Cervantes

A man may be a fool and not know it, but not if he is married.

HL Mencken

There is no need to fasten a bell to a fool.

Danish proverb

A learned fool is sillier than an ignorant one.

Molière

The fool has one great advantage over a man of sense - he is always satisfied with himself.

Napoleon Bonaparte

A fool never admires himself so much as when he has committed some folly.

Chinese proverb

Answer not the fool in his error, for thine attempts to instruct him will arouse his hatred.

Arabic proverb

A fellow who is always declaring he's no fool usually has his suspicions.

Wilson Mizner

Fool: someone who has been found out.

There was a time when a fool and his money were soon parted, but now it happens to everybody.

Adlai Stevenson

FORECASTING

It seems to me that no soothsayer should be able to look at another soothsayer without laughing.

Cicero

Predicting the future is, intellectually, the most disreputable form of public utterance.

Kenneth Clark

Man prefers to believe that which he prefers to be true.

Francis Bacon

The rule on staying alive as a financial forecaster is to give them a number or give them a date, but never give them both at once.

Business more than any other occupation is a continual dealing with the future: it is a continual calculation, an instinctive exercise in foresight.
You can only predict things after they have happened.

Eugène Ionesco

The only way to predict the future is to have power to shape the future.

FORGIVENESS

Forgotten is forgiven.

F Scott Fitzgerald

"I can forgive, but I cannot forget", is only another way of saying "I cannot forgive".

HW Beecher

God will pardon me; that's his business.

Heine

Don't carry a grudge. While you're carrying the grudge the other guy's out dancing.

Buddy Hackett

The weak can never forgive. Forgiveness is the attribute of the strong.

Mahatma Gandhi

Always forgive your enemies; nothing annoys them so much.

Oscar Wilde

It is manlike to punish, but godlike to forgive.

Peter von Winter

Bear and forbear.

FRIENDS

You learn in this business: if you want a friend, get a dog.

Carl Icahn

A friend is always happy about your success - if it doesn't surpass his own.

It is important to our friends to believe that we are unreservedly frank with them, and important to friendship that we are not.

Friendship is like a bank account. You can't continue to draw on it without making deposits.

The best way to lose a friend is to tell him something for his own good.

He is a good friend who speaks well of me behind my back.

Make new friends, but don't forget the old ones.
Yiddish proverb

A friend not in need is a friend indeed.

It is easier to forgive an enemy than to forgive a friend.

Every man should keep a fair-sized cemetery in which to bury the faults of his friends.

Friendship consists in forgetting what one gives and remembering what one receives.

If you want to make a dangerous man your friend, let him do you a favour.

That friendship will not continue to the end which is begun for an end.

A friend is someone whom we can always count on to count on us.

When you are down and out, something always turns up - and it's usually the noses of your friends.

Try your friend with a falsehood, and if he keeps it a secret, tell him the truth.
Italian proverb

A friend is someone who dislikes the same people that you dislike.

Prosperity makes friends and adversity tries them.

FUTURE

He who does not look ahead remains behind.
Spanish proverb

Remember, today is the tomorrow you worried about yesterday.
Dale Carnegie

The best way to be ready for the future is to invent it.
John Sculley

When all else is lost, the future still remains.

The future belongs to those who believe in the beauty of their dreams.
Eleanor Roosevelt

The future has a habit of suddenly and dramatically becoming the present.

The ability to plan for what has not yet happened, for a future that has only been imagined, is one of the hallmarks of leadership.

Your successful past will block your visions of the future.

I never think of the future. It comes soon enough.
Albert Einstein

Don't waste time looking back. Your eyes are in the front of your head.

The future is no longer what it used to be.

The future never just happened. It was created.

The trouble with the future is that it usually arrives before we are ready for it.

There is no future in any job. The future lies in the man who holds the job.

You can deal with the future more clearly if you don't focus on the next week.

It is futile to try to guess what products the future will want. But it is possible to make up one's mind what idea one wants to make a reality in the future, and to build a different business on such an idea.

Peter Drucker

If you do not think about the future, you cannot have one.

GAMBLING

The surest way of getting nothing for something.

Horse sense is what keeps horses from betting on what people will do.

The best throw of the dice is to throw them away.
English proverb

He who gambles picks his own pocket.

It may be that the race is not always to the swift, nor the battle to the strong - but that's the way to bet.
Damon Runyon

Without danger the game grows cold.

A wager is a fool's argument.
English proverb

There is scarcely an instance of a man who has made a fortune by speculation and kept it.
Andrew Carnegie

GENEROSITY

Less of your courtesy and more of your purse.
Scottish proverb

Lavishness is not generosity.
Thomas Fuller

Generosity consists not in the sum given, but the manner in which it is bestowed.

Generosity is the flower of justice.
Nathaniel Hawthorne

A small gift is better than a great promise.
German proverb

You never want to give a man a present when he's feeling good. You want to do it when he's down.

Lyndon B Johnson

To give and then not to feel that one has given is the very best of all ways of giving.

Max Beerbohm

There is a sublime thieving in all giving. Someone gives us all he has and we are his.

Eric Hoffer

Gifts are like hooks.

Martial

GENIUS

When a true genius appears in the world, you may know him by this sign, that the dunces are all in confederacy against him.

Jonathan Swift

The secret of genius is to carry the spirit of childhood into maturity.

TH Huxley

A genius is a talented person who does his homework.

Thomas Edison

In every work of genius we recognise our rejected thoughts.

Ralph Waldo Emerson

Talent does things tolerably well; genius does them intolerably better.

Since when was genius found respectable?

Elizabeth Barrett Browning

Doing easily what others find difficult is talent; doing what is impossible for talent is genius.

Henri Amiel

The function of genius is to furnish cretins with ideas twenty years later.

Louis Aragon

Patience is a necessary ingredient of genius.

Disraeli

No great genius has ever been without some madness.

Aristotle

GOALS

Before you can score you must first have a goal.

A goal is nothing more than a dream with a time limit.

Goals help you to overcome short-term problems.

Arriving at one's goal is the starting point to another.

Goal-setting is the strongest human force for self-motivation.

If you don't know where you are going, you might wind up somewhere else.

GOLDWYN GEMS
(Quotes attributed to immigrant studio boss Sam Goldwyn.)

A verbal contract isn't worth the paper it's written on.

That's the way with these directors, they're always biting the hand that lays the golden egg.

Our comedies are not to be laughed at.

It's more than magnificent, it's mediocre.

Let's have some new clichés.

Never let the bastard back into my room again - unless I need him.

What we need is a story that starts with an earthquake and works its way up to a climax.

We have all passed a lot of water since then.

I don't want any yes-men around me, I want everyone to tell me the truth even if it costs them their jobs.

I'll believe in colour television when I see it in black and white.

Tell me, how did you love my picture?

We're overpaying him, but he's worth it.

Gentlemen, include me out.

I had a terrific idea this morning, but I didn't like it.

Anyone who goes to a psychiatrist ought to have his head examined.

You've got to take the bull between your teeth.

GOLF

A handicapped golfer is a man who plays with his boss.

My golf is improving. Yesterday I hit the ball in one.

I could tell the previous speaker was a golfer by the way he held the mike with an interlocking grip.

Golf is so popular simply because it's the best game in the world at which to be bad.

AA Milne

The least thing upsets him on the links. He missed short putts because of the uproar of the butterflies in the adjoining meadows.

PG Wodehouse

I play golf in the low 80s. If it's any hotter than that, I won't play.

Joe E Lewis

In golf the ball always lies poorly; and the player well.

Golf is a good walk spoiled.

Mark Twain

Give me my golf clubs, fresh air and a beautiful partner, and you can keep my golf clubs and the fresh air.

Jack Benny

I have a bad swing, a bad stance and a bad grip, but my bank manager loves me.

Lee Trevino

Golf is like an eighteen-year-old girl with big boobs. You know it's wrong but you can't keep away from her.

I refuse to play golf with Errol Flynn. If I want to play with a prick, I'll play with my own.

WC Fields

Golf is the most popular way of beating around the bush.

What men do to relax when they are too tired to mow the lawn.

GOSSIP

Gossip is when you hear something you like about someone you don't.

Earl Wilson

I hate to spread rumours, but what else can you do with them?

Gossip is what you say about the objects of flattery when they aren't present.

PJ O'Rourke

I know that's a secret, for it is whispered everywhere.

William Congreve

There is only one thing in the world worse than being talked about, and that is not being talked about.

Oscar Wilde

A gossip tells things before you have a chance to tell them.

I will never repeat gossip, so please listen carefully the first time.

Whoever gossips to you will gossip of you.

Spanish proverb

Gossip always travels faster over grapevines that are slightly sour.

She has a nice sense of rumour.

None are so fond of secrets as those who do not mean to keep them.

Charles Colton

Don't forget to tell everyone it's a secret.

Gerald Lieberman

Some people believe everything you tell them....if you whisper it.

GOVERNMENT

Government should not interfere with any business capable of failing by itself.

Washington is a small town on the Potomac surrounded completely by reality.

George Will

Any man who thinks he is going to be happy and prosperous by letting the government take care of him should take a close look at the American Indian.

You don't see me at Vegas or at the races throwing my money around. I've got a government to support.

Bob Hope

To make crime unprofitable, let the government run it.

The natural progress of things is for government to gain ground and for liberty to yield.

Thomas Jefferson

When you think of the government debt the next generation must pay off, it's no wonder a baby yells when it is born.

Almost any system of government will work if the people will.

Useless laws weaken the necessary laws.

Govern a great nation as you would cook a small fish. Don't overdo it.

Lao-Tzu

The only thing that saves us from bureaucracy is its inefficiency.

There's no trick to being a humorist when you have the whole government working for you.

Will Rogers

The government solution to a problem is usually as bad as the problem.

Milton Friedman

A government that is big enough to give you all you want is big enough to take it all away.

Barry Goldwater

Many people consider the things government does for them to be social progress, but they regard the things government does for others as socialism.

Chief Justice Earl Warren

Whenever you have an efficient government you have a dictatorship.

Harry S Truman

GRATITUDE

The gratitude of most men is but a secret desire of receiving greater benefits.

La Rochefoucauld

Next to ingratitude, the most painful thing to bear is gratitude.

Henry Ward Beecher

Gratitude is a duty which ought to be paid, but which none has a right to expect.

Rousseau

Blessed is he who expects no gratitude, for he shall not be disappointed.

Nothing tires a man more than to be grateful all the time.

Gratitude is the conscience of memory.

Gratitude is a debt which usually goes on accumulating like blackmail; the more you pay, the more is exacted.

Mark Twain

GREED

If your desires be endless, your cares and fears will be so too.

Thomas Fuller

Big mouthfuls often choke.

Italian proverb

He would skin a flint.

John Berthelson

The covetous man is ever in want.

Horace

He is better with a rake than with a fork.

English proverb

I have one basic drive on my side they can't defeat - greed.

Frank Zappa

The entire essence of America is the hope to first make money - then make money with money - then make lots of money with lots of money.

Paul Erdman

GUESTS

A constant guest is never welcome.

English proverb

A guest sees more in an hour than the host in a year.

Polish proverb

My evening visitors, if they cannot see the clock should find the time in my face.

Ralph Waldo Emerson

When hospitality becomes an art, it loses its very soul.

Max Beerbohm

Killjoy was here.

Friendship increases in visiting friends, but in visiting them seldom.

Thomas Fuller

No one can be so welcome a guest that he will not annoy his host after three days.

Plautus

GUILT

He declares himself guilty who justifies himself before accusation.

Thomas Fuller

A guilty conscience is the mother of invention.

Carolyn Wells

The guilty think all talk is of themselves.

Chaucer

It is only too easy to compel a sensitive human being to feel guilty about anything.

Morton Irving Seiden

Everyone in daily life carries such a heavy, mixed burden of his own conscience that he is reluctant to penalise those who have been caught.

Brooks Atkinson

The offender never forgives.

Russian proverb

Guilt is always jealous.

A guilty conscience needs no accuser.

English proverb

HABIT

A shackle for the free.

Habits are first cobwebs, then cables.
Spanish proverb

Habits will reconcile us to everything but change.

Habit, if not resisted, soon becomes necessity.
St Augustine

One of the advantages of being disorderly is that one is constantly making exciting discoveries.
AA Milne

Forgive him, for he believes that the customs of his tribe are the laws of nature.
George Bernard Shaw

If you always do what you've always done, you'll always get what you've always got.
Ed Foreman

Habit creates the appearance of justice; progress has no greater enemy than habit.

Get in the habit of breaking your habits

Cultivate good habits - the bad ones all grow wild.

Men fall into a routine when they are tired and slack: it has all the appearance of activity with few of its burdens.
Walter Lippmann

HASTE

Whoever is in a hurry shows that the thing he is about is too big for him.
Lord Chesterfield

Make haste slowly.
Latin proverb

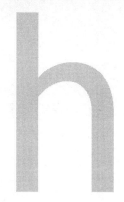

Three things only are well done in haste: flying from the plague, escaping quarrels, and catching fleas.
Russian proverb

He sows hurry and reaps indigestion.
Robert Louis Stevenson

One of the most pernicious effects of haste is obscurity.
Samuel Johnson

Haste makes waste.
English proverb

Hurry: a visible form of worry

HEROES

Show me a hero and I will write you a tragedy.
F Scott Fitzgerald

Every hero becomes a bore at last.
Ralph Waldo Emerson

We can't all be heroes because somebody has to sit on the curb and clap as they go by.
Will Rogers

The idol of today pushes the hero of yesterday out of our recollection; and will, in turn, be supplanted by his successor of tomorrow.
Washington Irving

Better not be a hero than work oneself up into heroism by shouting lies.
George Santayana

However great the advantages given us by nature, it is not she alone, but fortune with her, which makes heroes.
La Rochefoucald

The chief business of the nation, as a nation, is the setting up of heroes, mainly bogus.
HL Mencken

HIRING

Eagles don't flock - you have to find them one at a time.

Ross Perot

The best time to fire a person is before you hire them.

Everybody looks good on paper.

Don't bet on horses. Bet on jockeys.

Hiring is a manager's most important job.

Peter Drucker

I am always looking for people who can do a better job than I can.

T Boone Pickens

Never hire your client's children.

David Ogilvy

The first-rate man will try to surround himself with his equals, or betters if possible. The second-rate man will surround himself with third-rate men. The third-rate man will surround himself with fifth-rate men.

Andrew Weil

The employer generally gets the employees he deserves.

Sir Walter Bilbey

HOLIDAYS

If all the year were playing holidays
To sport would be as tedious as to work.

Shakespeare

A good holiday is one spent among people whose notions of time are vaguer than yours.

JB Priestley

A perpetual holiday is a good working definition of hell.

George Bernard Shaw

You must have been warned against letting the golden hours slip by. Yes, but some of them are golden only because we let them slip.

Sir James Barrie

I am happiest when I am idle. I could live for months without performing any kind of labour, and at the expiration of that time I should feel fresh and vigorous enough to go right on in the same way for numerous more months.

Artemus Ward

It is better to have loafed and lost than never to have loafed at all.

James Thurber

Leisure: time you spend on jobs you don't get paid for.

He does not seem to me a free man who does not sometimes do nothing.

Cicero

Leisure is the mother of philosophy.

Thomas Hobbes

One of the symptoms of approaching nervous breakdown is the belief that one's work is terribly important. If I were a medical man, I should prescribe a holiday to any patient who considered his work important.

Bertrand Russell

It is impossible to enjoy idling thoroughly unless one has plenty of work to do.

Jerome K Jerome

HOLLYWOOD

In Hollywood if you don't have a psychiatrist people think you are crazy.

Behind the phoney tinsel of Hollywood lies the real tinsel.

Oscar Levant

Hollywood is a place where people from Iowa mistake each other for stars.

Fred Allen

One producer was so impressed with the money made by *The Ten Commandments* that he hired a team of writers to come up with ten more.

In Hollywood they shoot too much film and not enough actors.

Hollywood is where, if you don't have happiness, you send out for it.

Rex Reed

Shoot a few scenes out of focus. I want you to win the foreign film award.

Billy Wilder, to a cameraman

Hollywood is an asylum run by the inmates.

In Hollywood, writers are considered only the first draft of human beings.

Hollywood is Disneyland staged by Dante. You imagine purgatory is like this except that the parking is not so good.

Robin Williams

Hollywood is a sewer - with services from the Ritz-Carlton.

Wilson Mizner

You can tell the economy is booming again. Yes-men in Hollywood are getting so independent they're only nodding.

Hollywood - a place where you spend more money than you make, on things you don't need, to impress people you don't like.

Ken Murray

HONESTY

A shady business never yields a sunny life.

It's strange that men should take up crime when there are so many legal ways to be dishonest.

The only disadvantage of an honest heart is credulity.

In business today, it's not the thief who can destroy a company. It's the honest man who doesn't know what the heck he's doing.

One cannot be a little dishonest - it's all the way or nothing.

If you are honest because you think that is the best policy, your honesty has already been corrupted.

It would be ingratitude in some men to turn honest when they owe all they have to their knavery.

I am afraid that we must make the world honest before we can honestly say to our children that honesty is the best policy.

George Bernard Shaw

h

Anger cannot be dishonest.

Honesty is a fine jewel, but much out of fashion.

Honesty is the best policy, but there are too few policyholders.

How desperately difficult it is to be honest with oneself. It is much easier to be honest with other people.

Edward F Benson

The liar's punishment is not in the least that he is not believed, but that he cannot believe anyone else.

George Bernard Shaw

Those who think it permissible to tell white lies soon grow colour-blind.

No man has a good enough memory to make a successful liar.

Abraham Lincoln

Tell your boss what you really think about him and the truth shall set you free.

HONOURS

Some are born great, some achieve greatness, and others have it pinned on them.

George Ade

It is better to deserve honours and not have them than to have them and not deserve them.

Mark Twain

When I want a peerage, I shall buy one like an honest man.

Lord Northcliffe

It is sure that those are most desirous of honour or glory who cry out loudest of its abuse and the vanity of the world.

Spinoza

Birds pay equal honours to all men.

English proverb

A king may make a nobleman, but he cannot make a gentleman.

Edmund Burke

Nobel Prize money is a lifebelt thrown to a swimmer who has already reached the shore in safety.

George Bernard Shaw

I don't deserve this, but then, I have arthritis and I don't deserve that either.

Jack Benny

Honour is better than honours.

Abraham Lincoln

HOPE

We should not let our fears hold us back from pursuing our hopes.

John F Kennedy

Hope, deceitful as it is, serves at least to lead us to the end of our lives by an agreeable route.

La Rochefoucauld

He fishes on who catches one.

French proverb

Hope for the best, but prepare for the worst.

English proverb

Hope is the poor man's bread.

At first we hope too much, later on, not enough.

Joseph Roux

Hope warps judgement in council, but quickens energy in action.

Bulwer-Lytton

There are no hopeless situations; there are only men who have grown hopeless about them.

h

Free hope from fear and
you become a dreamer.

Hope - desire and
expectation rolled into one.
Ambrose Bierce

He that does not hope to
win has already lost.

IDEAS

If you want to have a great idea, have lots of ideas.

If at first the idea is not absurd, then there is no hope for it.

Albert Einstein

Great ideas need landing gear as well as wings.

Many ideas grow better when transplanted into another mind than in the one where they sprang up.

Oliver Wendell Holmes

No army can withstand the strength of an idea whose time has come.

Victor Hugo

The idea that is not dangerous is not worthy of being called an idea at all.

If you want to get an idea across, wrap it up in a person.

To some people a bright idea is beginner's luck.

I could not sleep when I got on a hunt for an idea, until I had caught it; and when I thought I had got it, I was not satisfied until I had repeated it over and over again, until I had put it in language plain enough, as I thought, for any boy I knew to comprehend.

Abraham Lincoln

Ideas are the raw material of progress. Everything first takes shape in the form of an idea. But an idea by itself is worth nothing. An idea, like a machine, must have power applied to it before it can accomplish anything.

A new idea is delicate. It can be killed by a sneer or a yawn; it can be stabbed to death by a joke or worried to death by a frown on the right person's brow.

Every time a man puts a new idea across he finds ten men who thought of it before he did - but they only thought of it.

An idea isn't responsible for the people who believe in it.

It is better to entertain an idea than to take it home to live with you for the rest of your life.

No idea is so antiquated that it was not once modern.

No idea is so modern that it will not someday be antiquated.

Ellen Glasgow

A young man must let his ideas grow, not be continually rooting them up to see how they are getting on.

The only sure weapon against bad ideas is better ideas.

IMAGINATION

There are no days in life so memorable as those which vibrated to some stroke of the imagination.

Ralph Waldo Emerson

Imagination rules the world.

Napoleon Bonaparte

Reason can answer questions, but imagination has to ask them.

Ralph Gerrard

Imagination is more important than knowledge.

Albert Einstein

What is now proved was once only imagined.

William Blake

i

Imagination grows by exercise and contrary to common belief is more powerful in the mature than in the young.

Somerset Maugham

Imagination makes a man think he can run the business better than the boss.

His imagination resembled the wings of an ostrich. It enabled him to run, though not to soar.

Macaulay (of Dryden)

Anything one man can imagine, other men can make real.

Jules Verne

IMITATION

We are, in truth, more than half what we are by imitation.

Lord Chesterfield

The sense of inferiority inherent in the act of imitation breeds resentment. The impulse of the imitators is to overcome the model they imitate.

Eric Hoffer

Almost all absurdity of conduct arises from the imitation of those whom we cannot resemble.

Samuel Johnson

A man never knows what a fool he is until he hears himself imitated by one.

Sir Herbert Beerbohm Tree

We forfeit three-fourths of ourselves to be like other people.

Arthur Schopenhauer

It is better to fail in originality than to succeed in imitation.

Herman Melville

INDECISION

Nothing is so exhausting as indecision, and nothing is so futile.

Bertrand Russell

We know what happens to people who stay in the middle of the road. They get run over.

Aneurin Bevan

His indecision is final.

They call him "Jigsaw" because every time he's faced with a problem he goes to pieces.

Indecision is debilitating; it feeds upon itself; it is, one might almost say, habit forming. Not only that, but it is contagious; it transmits itself to others.

HA Hopf

Between two stools one sits on the ground.

French proverb

Nothing is more difficult, and therefore more precious, than to be able to decide.

Napoleon Bonaparte

Half the failures in life arise from pulling in one's horse as he is leaping.

I don't mind telling you exactly what I think. I'm undecided.

If you want to make decisions, then eliminate all the alternatives with the power of factual data. If you do not want to make decisions, then do us all a favour by staying out of the way.

One of these days is none of these days.

English proverb

I'd like to be a procrastinator, but I never seem to get around to it.
Chris Dundee

Procrastination is the thief of time.
Edward Young

Between saying and doing many a pair of shoes is worn out.
Italian proverb

INFLATION

Something similar to looking at your lifetime savings through the wrong end of a telescope.

A state of affairs when you never had it so good or parted with it so fast.

The reason you can't take it with you - it all goes before you do.

The time when people who used to say money isn't everything say it's hardly anything.

Being broke with a lot of money in your pocket.

You know inflation is out of hand when piggy banks cost more than they hold.

Inflation is a shot in the arm that leaves a pain in the neck.

One of the principal troubles about inflation is that the public likes it.
Lord Woolton

Think of the inflation spiral as a gigantic corkscrew - and think of yourself as the cork.

Inflation is another one of those problems that can't be cured by throwing money at it.

i

Inflation may have been arrested, as the economists claim, but whenever we go shopping it seems to be out on bail.

The cost of living is high, but it's worth it.

Inflation is the one form of taxation that can be imposed without legislation.

Milton Friedman

We have a love-hate relationship. We hate inflation, but we love everything that causes it.

Invest in inflation. It's the only thing going up.

Will Rogers

INHERITANCE

The art of will-making chiefly consists of baffling the importunity of expectation.

William Hazlitt

Nobody talks more of free enterprise and competition and of the best man winning than the man who has inherited his father's store or farm.

C Wright Mills

Say not you know another entirely till you have divided an inheritance with him.

He who inherits a penny is expected to spend a pound.

A son can bear with composure the death of his father, but the loss of his inheritance might drive him to despair.

Machiavelli

I am spending my children's inheritance.

It is a gorgeous gold pocket watch. I'm proud of it. My grandfather, on his death bed, sold me this watch.

Woody Allen

When you have told anyone you have left him a legacy, the only decent thing to do is to die at once.

Samuel Butler

INSURANCE

Something that costs you thousands of pounds so that when you are dead you'll have nothing to worry about.

Insurance people present plans to keep you poor while you are alive so that you may die rich.

In every insurance policy the big print giveth and the small print taketh away.

I thought my group insurance plan was fine until I found out that I couldn't collect unless the whole group is sick.

"Don't let me frighten you into making a hasty decision, Frank. Sleep on it tonight. If you wake up tomorrow, call me."

Insurance salesman: "Now that you are married, I'm sure that you will want to take on more insurance on yourself".
Young man: "I don't think I need any more. I don't think she's that dangerous".

He said it was a matter of life and death. It turned out he was an insurance salesman.

Buy an annuity cheap, and make your life interesting to yourself and everybody else that watches the speculation.

Charles Dickens

INTEGRITY

You don't turn integrity on and off. To have integrity you must be like the fellow who uses a butter knife when nobody is around.

The measure of a man's real character is what he would do if he knew he would never be found out.

Macaulay

I either want less corruption, or more chance to participate in it.

Ashleigh Brilliant

Character is doing what's right when nobody's looking.

Those are my principles. If you don't like them I have others.

Groucho Marx

Character is a victory, not a gift.

In matters of style, swim with the current; in matters of principle, stand like a rock.

Thomas Jefferson

Ethics stay in the preface of the average business science book.

Peter Drucker

I ran the wrong kind of business, but I did it with integrity.

Sydney Biddle Barrows

You cannot drive straight on a twisting road.

Russian proverb

Nothing so completely baffles one who is full of trick and duplicity himself, than straightforward and simple integrity in another.

Charles Colton

INVENTIONS

We are more ready to try the untried when what we do is inconsequential. Hence the remarkable fact that many inventions had their birth as toys.

Eric Hoffer

Inventor: a person who makes an ingenious arrangement of wheels, levers and springs, and believes it civilisation.

Ambrose Bierce

Inventor: an old-fashioned creator almost entirely supplanted by research and development departments.

We owe a lot to Thomas Edison - if it wasn't for him, we'd be watching television by candlelight.

Milton Berle

Inventors and men of genius have almost always been regarded as fools at the beginning (and very often at the end) of their careers.

Dostoevsky

Name the greatest of all the inventors. Accident.

Mark Twain

INVESTING

If you see a bandwagon, it's too late.

James Goldsmith

Buy when everyone else is selling and hold until everyone else is buying. This is not merely a catchy slogan. It is the very essence of successful investment.

J Paul Getty

i

Investing is not as tough as being a top-notch bridge player. All it takes is the ability to see things as they really are.

Warren Buffett

It's a good deal easier to know what's going to happen than when it's going to happen.

There are two times in a man's life when he should not speculate in stocks; when he can't afford it, and when he can.

Mark Twain

When you look at a stock you already own ask yourself every day: "Would I buy this stock today?" If the answer is yes, then hold on or buy more. If the answer is no, then sell regardless of the value of the stock.

Bernard Baruch

How did I make my fortune? By always selling too soon.

Nathan Rothschild

Better to lose the anchor than the whole ship.

I've been burned in the stock market by picking up a hot tip.

People who play the market are often led astray by false profits.

The only difference between the current stock market and the Titanic is that the Titanic had a band.

I made a killing in the stock market. I shot my broker.

A friend in need is a friend who has been playing the stock market.

Buy land. They've stopped making it.

Mark Twain

I'm only working because of an accident. I got hit by a falling stock market.

Never invest your money in anything that eats or needs repainting.

Billy Rose

There is nothing so disastrous as a rational investment policy in an irrational world.

John Maynard Keynes

Fools rush in where angels fear to trade.

Old men are always advising young men to save money. That is bad advice. Don't save every nickel. Invest in yourself. I never saved a dollar until I was forty years old.

Henry Ford

Put all your eggs in one basket and then watch that basket.

Mark Twain

The bulls make money. The bears make money. But the pigs get slaughtered.

Wall Street axiom

JUDGEMENT

The good judgement of some people will never wear out. They don't use it often enough.

We judge ourselves by what we feel capable of doing; others judge us by what we have done.

Longfellow

Enthusiasm for a cause sometimes warps judgement.

William Howard Taft

Most people suspend their judgement till somebody else has expressed his own and then they repeat it.

Ernest Dimnet

Everyone complains of his memory, but no-one complains of his judgement.

The ultimate cynicism is to suspend judgement so that you are not judged.

Marya Mannes

Knowledge is the treasure, but judgement the treasurer of a wise man.

William Penn

A hasty judgement is the first step to recantation.

KNOWLEDGE

The person who knows everything has the most to learn.

To be conscious that you are ignorant is a great step to knowledge.
Benjamin Disraeli

A little learning is a dangerous thing.
Alexander Pope

Knowledge is power.

He that knows little often repeats it.

Even a professor soon discovers how little he knows when a child begins asking questions.

We are drowning in information but starved for knowledge.
John Naisbitt

The secret of business is to know something that nobody else knows.
Aristotle Onassis

You never have to know all the answers because you won't be asked all the questons.

You can know ten things by learning one.
Japanese proverb

You can always spot a well-informed man - his views are the same as yours.

Nothing annoys me more than a man who thinks he knows it all - and does.

The important thing is not to know more than all men, but to know more at each moment than any particular man.

As knowledge increases, wonder deepens.

k

Knowledge and timber shouldn't be much used till they are seasoned.

Everything I know about this subject would fit into a nutshell and still leave plenty of room for the nut.

Lord Mancroft

If a little knowledge is dangerous, where is the man who has so much as to be out of danger?

TH Huxley

Many shall run to and fro, and knowledge shall be increased.

Old Testament

A man should keep his little brain attic stocked with all the furniture that he is likely to use, and the rest he can put away in the lumber room of his library, where he can get it if he wants it.

Sir Arthur Conan Doyle

In order that knowledge be properly digested, it must have been swallowed with a good appetite.

Anatole France

If we value the pursuit of knowledge, we must be free to follow wherever that search may lead us. The free mind is no barking dog, to be tethered on a ten-foot chain.

Adlai Stevenson

Many men are stored full of unused knowledge. Like loaded guns that are never fired off, or military magazines in times of peace, they are stuffed with useless ammunition.

Henry Ward Beecher

LANGUAGE AND LANGUAGES

I speak Spanish to God, Italian to women, French to men, and German to my horse.

Charles V

English is a funny language. A fat chance and a slim chance are the same thing.

"Basta!" his master replied, with all the brilliant glibness of the Berlitz school.

Ronald Firbank

In Paris they simply stared when I spoke to them in French; I never did succeed in making those idiots understand their own language.

Mark Twain

Slang is a language that rolls up its sleeves, spits on its hands and goes to work.

Carl Sandburg

The great enemy of clear language is insincerity. When there is a gap between one's real and one's declared aims one turns as it were instinctively to long words and exhausted idioms, like cuttlefish squirting out ink.

George Orwell

LAWYERS

The first thing we do, let's kill all the lawyers.

Shakespeare

Lawyers sometimes tell the truth - they'll do anything to win a case.

A poor man between two lawyers is like a fish between two cats.

It is a secret worth knowing that lawyers rarely go to law.

A lawyer is a man who profits by your experience.

Laws are made to trouble people, and the more trouble they make the longer they stay on the statute books.

A lawyer is a learned gentleman who rescues your estate from your enemies and keeps it himself.

Lord Brougham

When there is no will there is a way for the lawyers.

Woe be to him whose advocate becomes his accuser.

A society of men bred up from their youth in the art of proving by words multiplied for the purpose that white is black and black is white according as they are paid.

Jonathan Swift

Lawyers' houses are built on the heads of fools.

English proverb

I would be loth to speak ill of any person who I do not know deserves it, but I am afraid that he is an attorney.

Samuel Johnson

Laws, like houses, lean on one another.

Edmund Burke

The robes of lawyers are lined with the obstinacy of clients.

English proverb

It is the trade of lawyers to question everything, yield nothing, and to talk by the hour.

Thomas Jefferson

Only painters and lawyers can change white to black.

Japanese proverb

A lawyer is someone who will read a 10,000-word document and call it a brief.

Talk is cheap - if lawyers don't do the talking.

Lawyers make a living trying to figure out what other lawyers have written.

Will Rogers

My definition of utter waste is a coachload of lawyers going over a cliff with three empty seats.

Lamar Hunt

I get paid for seeing that my clients have every break the law allows. I have knowingly defended a number of guilty men. But the guilty never escape unscathed. My fees are sufficient punishment for anyone.

F Lee Bailey

If I were to give you an orange I'd simply say: "I give you this orange". But when the transaction is entrusted to a lawyer he puts down: "I hereby give and convey to you all and singular, my estate and interests, rights, title, claim and advantages of and in said orange, together with all its rind, juice, pulp and pips and all rights and advantages with full power to bite, cut and otherwise eat the same, or give the same away with or without the rind, skin, juice, pulp or pips, anything herein before and herein after or in any other deed, or deeds, instruments of whatever nature or kind whatsoever to the contrary in anywise notwithstanding............." Then a couple of smart lawyers come along and take it away from you.

My son works for a law firm. He makes loopholes.

LEADERSHIP

A leader takes people where they want to go. A good leader takes people where they don't necessarily want to go but ought to be.

One of the tests of leadership is the ability to recognise a problem before it becomes an emergency.

People buy into the leader before they buy into the vision.

Leadership is the ability to decide what is to be done and then to get others to want to do it.
Dwight D Eisenhower

There are no bad soldiers, only bad officers.
Napoleon Bonaparte

Without a shepherd, sheep are not a flock.
Russian proverb

It is always a great mistake to command when you are not sure you will be obeyed.
Honoré, Comte de Mirabeau

There is no trick to being a captain as long as the sea is calm.

A good leader can't get too far ahead of his followers.
FD Roosevelt

Something is happening in our country. We aren't producing leaders like we used to. A new chief executive officer today, exhausted by the climb to the peak, falls down on the mountaintop and goes to sleep.

Robert Townsend

You manage things; you lead people.

The graveyards are full of indispensable men.

Charles de Gaulle

A good leader is a person who takes a little more than his share of the blame and a little less than his share of the credit.

Keep you fears to yourself, but share your courage with others.

Robert Louis Stevenson

For if the trumpet give an uncertain sound, who shall prepare himself to the battle?

Bible

The final test of a leader is the feeling that you have when you leave his presence after a conference. Have you a feeling of uplift and confidence?

Field Marshal Montgomery

You do not lead by hitting people over the head - that's assault, not leadership.

Dwight D Eisenhower

I must follow them. I am their leader.

Andrew Bonar Law, former Conservative Prime Minister

If you've got them by the balls, their hearts and minds will follow.

Lyndon B Johnson

Men will follow him anywhere - out of curiosity.

A leader is a dealer in hope.
Napoleon Bonaparte

The leader, mingling with the vulgar host, is in the common mass of matter lost.
Homer

The weakness of the many makes the leader possible.
Elbert Hubbard

LETTERS

I have made this letter longer than usual because I haven't had time to make it shorter.
Pascal

A man seldom puts his authentic self into a letter. He writes it to amuse a friend or to get rid of a social or business obligation, which is to say, a nuisance.
HL Mencken

One of the pleasures of reading old letters is the knowledge that they need no answer.
Lord Byron

The great secret in life is not to open your letters for a fortnight. At the expiration of that period you will find that nearly all of them have answered themselves.
Arthur Binstead

They prosper who burn in the morning the letters they wrote overnight.

LUCK

Luck seems to have a peculiar attachment to work.

A rabbit's foot may be lucky, but the original owner wasn't.

The only sure thing about luck is that it will change.

Throw a lucky man into the sea, and he will come up with a fish in his mouth.

Arab proverb

The only good luck many great men ever had was being born with the ability and determination to overcome bad luck.

It often amazes me to hear men impute all their misfortune to fate, luck, or destiny, whilst their successes or good fortune they ascribe to their own sagacity, cleverness, or penetration.

Samuel Taylor Coleridge

Good luck is a lazy man's estimate of a worker's success.

A pound of pluck is worth a ton of luck.

Luck never made a man wise.

Seneca

Not a man alive has so much luck that he can play with it.

William Butler Yeats

Luck is not something you can mention in the presence of self-made men.

EB White

If it weren't for bad luck I wouldn't have any luck at all.

Dick Gregory

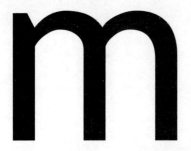

MANAGEMENT

Good management consists in showing average people how to do the work of superior people.

John D Rockefeller

It's easy to get good players. Getting them to play together, that's the hard part.

Most business failures do not stem from bad times. They come from poor management, and bad times just precipitate the crisis.

There are times when even the best manager is like the little boy with the big dog waiting to see where the dog wants to go so he can take him there.

Lee Iacocca

If you can't get people to accept ideas because they're sound, and if you are not willing to accept an idea because it's sound, then you're really not a good manager.

Managers: people who take responsibility when things go right.

Lots of people confuse bad management with destiny.

So much of what we call management consists in making it difficult for people to work.

Peter Drucker

MARKETING

Marketing is an attitude, not a department.

A man's success in business today depends upon his power of getting people to believe he has something they want.

The only way to convert a heathen is to travel into the jungle.

Marketing is creating a condition that allows the buyer to convince himself to buy.

A good marketing strategy is to find a gap in a market that already exists.

There is more similarity in the marketing challenge of selling a precious painting by Degas and a frosted mug of root beer than you ever thought possible.
Alfred Taubman (owner of Sotheby's)

MEASUREMENT

I am one of those unpraised, unrewarded millions without whom statistics would be a bankrupt science. It is we who are born, who marry, who die, in constant ratios.
Logan Pearsall Smith

Not everything that counts can be counted, and not everything that can be counted, counts.

You can't measure the whole world with your own yardstick.
Yiddish proverb

Never measure the height of a mountain until you have reached the top. Then you will see how low it was.
Dag Hammarskjöld

He uses statistics as a drunken man uses lamp-posts - for support rather than illumination.

Statistician: a man who draws a mathematically precise line from an unwarranted assumption to a foregone conclusion.

There are no facts, only interpretations.

Nietzsche

Statistics are like loose women; once you get your hands on them you can do anything you like with them.

Smoking is one of the leading causes of statistics.

Statistics are like a bikini. What they reveal is suggestive, but what they conceal is vital.

Aaron Levenstein

There are two kinds of statistics, the kind you look up and the kind you make up.

Rex Stout

MEDICINE AND DOCTORS

It is a poor doctor who cannot prescribe an expensive cure for a rich patient.

Sydney Tremayne

One doctor makes work for another.

We've made great medical progress in the last generation. What used to be merely an itch is now an allergy.

Mary had a little lamb. The doctor fainted.

Asthma is a disease that has practically the same symptoms as passion, except that with asthma it lasts longer.

A psychiatrist is a man who asks you a lot of expensive questions your wife asks you for nothing.

Show me a sane man and I will cure him for you.

Carl Jung

The art of medicine consists in amusing the patient while Nature effects the cure.

Voltaire

There's another advantage to being poor - a doctor will cure you faster.

Kim Hubbard

The desire to take medicine is perhaps the greatest feature which distinguishes man from animals.

William Osler

Our doctor would never really operate unless it was absolutely necessary. He was just that way. If he didn't need the money, he wouldn't lay a hand on you.

Herb Shriner

Some doctors tell their patients the worst - others mail them the bill.

Doctors are becoming easier to find these days. Most of the caddies have portable phones.

The physician must have at his command a certain ready wit, as dourness is repulsive both to the healthy and to the sick.

Hippocrates

Only a fool will make a doctor his heir.

Russian proverb

A minor operation: one performed on somebody else.

The purse of the patient protracts his cure.

MEETINGS

Meetings are indispensable when you don't want to do anything.

John Kenneth Galbraith

Why do we take notes of meetings that last for hours and call them minutes?

Show me a person who likes to go to meetings and I'll show you a person who doesn't have enough to do.

I always come to meetings with a problem. I always leave with a briefing and a problem.

A conference is a gathering of important people who singly can do nothing but together can decide that nothing can be done.

Every discussion in a meeting has a diminishing curve of interest. The longer the discussion goes on, the fewer people will be interested in it.

Mark McCormack

Conferences are primarily a means of enabling people with some common interests to present a united front against the outside world.

If a manager spends more than 25 per cent of his time in meetings it is a sign of poor organisation.

Peter Drucker

Conference: a meeting at which people talk about what they should be doing.

You know, if an orange and an apple went into conference consultations, it might come out a pear.

Ronald Reagan

Parkinson's Law of Triviality: The time spent on any item on the agenda will be in inverse proportion to the sum involved.

C Northcote Parkinson

The reason that everybody likes planning is that nobody has to do anything.

Governor Jerry Brown

MEMORY

To improve your memory, lend people money.

Writing things down is the best secret of a good memory.

The true art of memory is the art of attention.

How sweet to remember the trouble that is past!

We do not remember days, we remember moments.

We have all forgot more than we remember.

Not the power to remember, but its very opposite, the power to forget, is a necessary condition for our existence.

How strange are the tricks of memory, which, often hazy as a dream about the most important things of a man's life, religiously preserve the merest of trifles.

Sir Richard Burton

I have a memory like an elephant. In fact, elephants often consult me.

Noël Coward

Memory is the diary that we all carry about with us.

Oscar Wilde

MISTAKES

He who never made a mistake never made a discovery.

Samuel Smiles

Stumbling is not falling.

Portuguese proverb

The greatest mistake you can make in this life is to be continually fearing you will make one.

It doesn't matter how much milk you spill just so long as you don't lose your cow.

Old Texas saying

The causes of mistakes are first, "I didn't know"; second, "I didn't think"; third, "I didn't care".

No matter how desperate the predicament is, I am always very much in earnest about clutching my cane, straightening my derby and fixing my tie even though I have just landed on my head.

Charlie Chaplin

Henry Ford forgot to put a reverse gear in his first car.

A doctor can bury his mistakes but an architect can only advise his clients to plant vines.

Frank Lloyd Wright

Mistakes are often the best teachers. The shortest mistakes are always the best.

French proverb

Any man may make a mistake; none but a fool will persist in it.

Latin proverb

It is very easy to forgive others their mistakes. It takes more guts and gumption to forgive them for having witnessed your own.

Things could be worse. Suppose your errors were counted and published every day, like those of a baseball player.

Wise men learn by other men's mistakes, fools by their own.

MONEY

Money talks, but it doesn't always make sense.

The only substance which can keep a cold world from calling a citizen: "Hey you!".

That element which makes stupidity shine.

The best passport.

The best tranquilliser.

The most effective labour-saving device.

The theatre's sweet music.

Money can't buy everything - poverty, for example.

By the time a man has money to burn, the fire has gone out.

When money speaks the truth is silent.
Russian proverb

With money in your pocket you are wise, and you are handsome, and you sing well too.
Yiddish proverb

Money talks. It says goodbye.

If you would know the value of money, go and try to borrow some.

Money often costs too much.

Lack of money is the root of all evil.

It is easier to make money than to keep it.
Yiddish proverb

If only God would give me a clear sign - like making a large deposit in my name in a Swiss bank!
Woody Allen

When I had money everyone called me brother.
Polish proverb

A heavy purse makes a light heart.

If a man's after money, he's moneymad; if he keeps it, he's a capitalist; if he spends it, he's a playboy. If he doesn't get it, he's a ne'er-do-well; if he doesn't try to get it, he lacks ambition. If he gets it without working for it, he's a parasite; and if he accumulates it after a lifetime of hard work people call him a fool who never got anything out of life.

A money-grabber is anyone who grabs more money than you can.

When I was young I used to think that money was the most important thing in life; now that I am old, I know it is.
Oscar Wilde

The nicest thing about money is that it never clashes with anything I wear.

I don't like money actually, but it quiets my nerves.

Joe Louis

I have enough money to last me the rest of my life, unless I buy something.

Put not your trust in money, but put your money in trust.

There'll be no pockets in your shroud.

O, what a world of vile ill-favour'd faults look handsome in three hundred pounds a year!

Shakespeare

Some people think they are worth a lot of money because they have it.

When a fellow says "It isn't the money but the principle of the thing" - it's the money.

Don't marry for money; you can borrow it cheaper.

Scottish proverb

My problem lies in reconciling my gross habits with my net income.

Errol Flynn

I'm living so far beyond my income that we might be said to be living apart.

Saving is a very fine thing, especially if your parents have done it for you.

Winston Churchill

Money won't buy happiness, but it will pay the salaries of a large research staff to study the problem.

Money isn't everything; usually it isn't even enough.

All right, so I like spending money! But name any other extravagance!

Max Kauffmann

NECESSITY

Necessity makes even the timid brave.

Necessity relieves us from the embarrassment of choice.

Necessity is a hard nurse, but she raises strong children.

Necessity never made a good bargain.

Necessity turns lion into fox.

Persian proverb

Necessity, the mother of invention.

Necessity is the plea for every infringement of human freedom. It is the argument of tyrants; it is the creed of slaves.

William Pitt

Where necessity speaks it demands.

Russian proverb

NEGOTIATION

Don't slam the door; you might want to go back.

When I'm getting ready to reason with a man I spend one-third of my time thinking about myself and what I am going to say - and two-thirds about him and what he is going to say.

Abraham Lincoln

A lot of times you can push someone to the wall, and you still reach agreement, but his resentment will come back to haunt you in a million ways.

Mark McCormack

In a successful negotiation everybody wins.

Always deal with the person who signs the cheques.

When a man tells me he's going to put all his cards on the table, I always look up his sleeve.

Lord Hore-Belisha

Nothing astonishes men so much as common sense and plain dealing.

Ralph Waldo Emerson

My style of dealmaking is quite simple and straightforward. I just keep pushing and pushing and pushing to get what I'm after.

Donald Trump

NEWS AND NEWSPAPERS

It's not the world that's got so much worse but the news coverage that's got so much better.

GK Chesterton

Everything you read in the newspapers is absolutely true except for the rare story of which you happen to have first-hand knowledge.

Erwin Knoll

The evil that men do lives on the front pages of greedy newspapers, but the good is often interred apathetically inside.

Brooks Atkinson

If some great catastrophe is not announced every morning, we feel a certain void. "Nothing in the paper today", we sigh.

Paul Valéry

He had been kicked in the head by a mule when young, and believed everything he read in the Sunday papers.

George Ade

Journalism largely consists of saying "Lord Jones Dead" to people who never knew that Lord Jones was alive.

GK Chesterton

An editor is one who separates the wheat from the chaff and prints the chaff.

Adlai Stevenson

I read the newspapers avidly. It is my one form of continuous fiction.

Aneurin Bevan

I'm with you on the free press. It's the newspapers I can't stand.

Tom Stoppard

Four hostile newspapers are more to be feared than a thousand bayonets.

Napoleon Bonaparte

I keep reading between the lies.

Goodman Ac

No news is good news.

Italian prover

OPPORTUNITY

When the sun rises, it rises for everyone.

If opportunity doesn't knock, build a door.

Ability is nothing without opportunity.
Napoleon Bonaparte

The dawn does not come twice to awaken a man.
Arabic proverb

When written in Chinese, the word "crisis" is composed of two characters. One represents danger and the other represents opportunity.

Small opportunities are often the beginnings of great enterprises.

I was seldom able to see an opportunity until it had ceased to be one.
Mark Twain

No great man ever complains of want of opportunity.
Ralph Waldo Emerson

Opportunity is missed by most people because it is dressed in overalls and looks like work.
Thomas Edison

Even when opportunity knocks, a man must get off his seat to open the door.

When opportunity knocks, most people are out in the backyard looking for four-leaf clovers.

If you're looking for a big opportunity, seek out a big problem.

Not only strike while the iron is hot, but make it hot by striking.
Oliver Cromwell

A wise man will make more opportunities than he finds.

Francis Bacon

There is no security on this earth; there is only opportunity.

Douglas MacArthur

OPTIMISM

A cheerful frame of mind that enables a kettle to sing though in hot water up to its nose.

Keep your face to the sunshine and you cannot see the shadow.

In the long run the pessimist may be proved to be right, but the optimist has a better time on the trip.

The doctrine of belief that everything is beautiful, including what is ugly.

An optimist is a fellow who believes what's going to be will be postponed.

A mania for maintaining that all is well when things are going badly.

Voltaire

Optimist: a man who sets aside two hours to do his income tax return.

Since the house is on fire let us warm ourselves.

Italian saying

An optimist is a man who, instead of feeling sorry that he cannot pay his bills, is glad he is not one of his creditors.

An optimist is someone who tells you to cheer up when things are going his way.

p

PAPERWORK

Too many people are like Samuel Goldwyn, who said: "I read part of it all the way through".

A memorandum is written not to inform the reader but to protect the writer.

Dean Acheson

The volume of paper expands to fill the available briefcases.

Governor Jerry Brown

If you don't know what to do with many of the papers piled on your desk, stick a dozen colleagues' initials on them and pass them along. When in doubt, route.

Malcolm Forbes

PAST

In every age "the good old days" were a myth. No-one ever thought they were good at the time. For every age has consisted of crises that seemed intolerable to the people that lived through them.

Brooks Atkinson

Nothing is more responsible for the good old days than a bad memory.

Franklin P Adams

The golden age was never the present age.

English proverb

Every age has a keyhole to which its eye is pasted.

Mary McCarthy

The "good old times" - all times, when old, are good.

Lord Byron

No man is rich enough to buy back his past.

Oscar Wilde

In the carriages of the past you can't go anywhere.

Maxim Gorky

Why doesn't the past decently bury itself, instead of sitting waiting to be admired by the present?

DH Lawrence

It's futile to talk too much about the past - something like trying to make birth control retroactive.

Charles Edward Wilson

History teaches us that men and nations behave wisely once they have exhausted all other alternatives.

Abba Eban

PATIENCE

A minor form of despair, disguised as virtue.

Lord grant me patience, and I want it right now.

He preacheth patience that never knew pain.

It is easy to find reasons why other folks should be patient.

Patience is bitter, but its fruit is sweet.

French proverb

Patience, the beggar's virtue.

That which in mean men we entitle patience
Is pale cold cowardice in noble breasts.

Shakespeare

Patience is the virtue of an ass, that trots beneath its burdens, and is quiet.

Be patient; in time even an egg will walk.

African proverb

A handful of patience is worth more than a bushel of brains.

Dutch proverb

Nothing is so full of victory as patience.

Chinese proverb

Patience is a most necessary quality for business: many a man would rather you heard his story than granted his request.

Earl of Chesterfield

PERSEVERANCE

Many strokes overthrow the tallest oak.

Nothing in the world can take the place of persistence.

Calvin Coolidge

Success seems to be largely a matter of hanging on after others have let go.

Victory belongs to the most persevering.

Napoleon Bonaparte

Diligence is the mother of good luck.

Fall seven times, stand up eight.

Japanese proverb

The difference between perseverance and obstinacy is that one comes from a strong will and the other from a strong won't.

There are no traffic jams when you go the extra mile.

PERSUASION

By persuading others, we convince ourselves.

Soft words are hard arguments.

p

You can get much farther with a kind word and a gun than with a kind word alone.

Al Capone

People are generally better persuaded by the reasons which they have themselves discovered than by those which come into the minds of others.

Pascal

If you can engage people's pride, love, pity, ambition (or whatever is their prevailing passion) on your side you need not fear what their reason can do against you.

Lord Chesterfield

Few are open to conviction, but the majority of men are open to persuasion.

Goethe

PESSIMISM

Scratch a pessimist, and you find often a defender of privilege.

Lord Beveridge

Pessimism is the triumph of worry over matter.

Pessimism is a sickness you treat like any other sickness. The object is to get well of it as soon as possible, and get back to business.

Aristotle Onassis

To believe a thing impossible is to make it so.

French proverb

Man who says it cannot be done should not interrupt man doing it.

Chinese proverb

Cheer up. The worst is yet to come.

A PESSIMIST IS:

One who, when he has the choice of two evils, chooses both.

A man with a difficulty for every solution.

A person who looks both ways before crossing a one-way street.

Someone who can look at the land of milk and honey and see only calories and cholesterol.

A man who financed an optimist.

A person who, when smelling flowers, looks around for the funeral.

A person to borrow money from - he never expects to be repaid.

A pessimist is a man who thinks all women are bad. An optimist is one who hopes they are.

PLANNING

Make no little plans; they have no magic to stir men's blood.
Daniel Burnham

Do not plan for ventures before finishing what's at hand.

It is a bad plan that admits of no modification.

Plans get you into things but you got to work your way out.
Will Rogers

People who fail to plan, have planned to fail.

Long-range planning does not deal with future decisions, but with the future of present decisions.
Peter Drucker

Dig a well before you are thirsty.
Chinese proverb

When schemes are laid in advance, it is surprising how often the circumstances fit in with them.

Sir William Osler

Chance favours only the prepared mind.

Louis Pasteur

Men never plan to be failures; they simply fail to plan to be successful.

William A Ward

POLITICS

Practical politics consists in ignoring facts.

Henry Adams

Lincoln was right, of course; you can't fool all of the people all of the time; but you only have to fool a majority.

Politics: the gentle art of getting votes from the poor and campaign funds from the rich, by promising to protect each from the other.

Oscar Ameringer

Politicians are the same all over. They promise to build a bridge even when there is no river.

Nikita Khrushchev

A politician is an animal that can sit on a fence and keep both ears to the ground.

HL Mencken

The most successful politician is he who says what everybody is thinking most often and in a loud voice.

Theodore Roosevelt

Being in politics is like being a football coach. You have to be smart enough to understand the game and stupid enough to think it's important.

Eugene McCarthy

An honest politician is one who, when he is bought, will stay bought.

Simon Cameron

Probably the most distinctive characteristic of the successful politician is selective cowardice.

Richard Harris

If you want to succeed in politics, you must keep your conscience well under control.

David Lloyd George

Have you ever seen a candidate talking to a rich person on television?

Art Buchwald

We all know that Prime Ministers are wedded to the truth, but like other wedded couples they sometimes live apart.

HH Munro

There's just one rule for politicians all over the world: don't say in power what you say in opposition. If you do, you only have to carry out what the other fellows have found impossible.

John Galsworthy

He knows nothing and he thinks he knows everything. That clearly points to a political career.

George Bernard Shaw

Politics: a strife of interests masquerading as a contest of principles.

Ambrose Bierce

POVERTY

The easiest way to remain poor is to pretend to be rich.

It is easier to praise poverty than to bear it.

I wasn't born in a log cabin, but my family moved into one as soon as they could afford it.

Melville D Landon

Honest poverty is a gem that even a king might be proud to call his own, but I wish to sell out.

Mark Twain

We who are liberal and progressive know that the poor are our equals in every sense except that of being equal to us.

Lionel Trilling

The trouble with being poor is that it takes up all your time.

Willem de Kooning

An empty purse frightens away friends.

Thomas Fuller

The rich would have to eat money, but luckily the poor provide food.

Russian proverb

Empty pockets make empty heads.

William Carlos Williams

Poverty is no disgrace, but no honour either.

Yiddish proverb

Look at me. Worked myself up from nothing to a state of extreme poverty.

SJ Perelman

The most inconvenient feature about poverty is that one is apt to get used to it.

The poor are rightfully the property of the rich, because the rich made them.

It is the weariness of the poor that keeps the rich in power.

Poverty: the condition we try to conceal at the time and then brag about in our memoirs.

FG Kerman

POWER

Lust of power is the strongest of all passions.

Latin proverb

Nearly all men can stand adversity, but if you want to test a man's character, give him power.

Abraham Lincoln

I'm caught in a power struggle. My boss has the power and I have the struggle.

Power is the ability to make changes.

When I make a movie I am like God. I have the world in my hands. I make it come out any way I want, decide who lives and who dies, who gets punished, who gets to live happily ever after. In between pictures is my seventh day, I rest.

John Huston

Those who have been once intoxicated with power, and have derived any kind of emolument from it, even though but for one year, can never willingly abandon it.

Edmund Burke

A friend in power is a friend lost.

Henry Adams

The pursuit of power explains most human behaviour.

Nietzsche

Power can corrupt, but absolute power is absolutely delightful.

We thought because we had power we had wisdom.
Stephen Vincent Benet

Our sense of power is more vivid when we break a man's spirit than when we win his heart.
Eric Hoffer

Power, when exercised over matter or over man, is partial to simplification.

A cock has great influence on his own dunghill.

The eagle suffers little birds to sing.
Shakespeare

If you would be powerful, pretend to be powerful.
Horne Took

PRAISE AND FLATTERY

Praise undeserved is satire in disguise.

I suppose flattery hurts no-one, that is, if he doesn't inhale.
Adlai Stevenson

What really flatters a man is that you think him worth flattering.
George Bernard Shaw

Some people pay a compliment as if they expected a receipt.
Kim Hubbard

None are more apt to praise others extravagantly than those who desire to be praised themselves.

Get someone else to blow your horn and the sound will carry twice as far.
Will Rogers

p

One catches more flies with a spoonful of honey than with twenty casks of vinegar.
French proverb

Flattery never comes up to the expectancy of conceit.

Compliments cost nothing, yet many pay dear for them.

I didn't hear all the boss said - I was on my knees at the time.

A "Yes man" is a guy who kisses his boss on all cheeks.

He who knows how to flatter also knows how to slander.
Napoleon Bonaparte

Flattery is a base coin which is current only through our vanity.

The advantage of doing one's praising to oneself is that one can lay it on so thick and exactly in the right places.
Samuel Butler

Praise makes good men better and bad men worse.
Thomas Fuller

Praises from an enemy imply real merit.

There's no praise to beat the sort you can put in your pocket.
Molière

We begin to praise when we begin to see a thing needs our assistance.
Thoreau

If you can't think of any other way to flatter a man, tell him he's the kind of man who can't be flattered.

p

Flattery is the art of telling another person exactly what he thinks of himself.

PREJUDICE

Prejudice is a great time-saver. You can form opinions without having to get the facts.

The difference between a prejudice and a conviction is that you can explain a conviction without getting mad.

We hate some persons because we do not know them; and we will not know them because we hate them.

Charles Coulton

Prejudice is the child of ignorance.

William Hazlitt

Everyone is a prisoner of his own experiences. No-one can eliminate prejudices - just recognise them.

Edward R Murrow

The tendency of the casual mind is to pick out or stumble upon a sample which supports or defies its prejudices, and then to make it representative of a whole class.

Walter Lippmann

A prejudice is a vagrant opinion without any visible means of support.

Ambrose Bierce

He who never leaves his country is full of prejudices.

Goldoni

PRIDE

What the world needs is more geniuses with humility. There are so few of us left.

Oscar Levant

If a proud man makes me keep my distance, the comfort is that he keeps his at the same time.

Jonathan Swift

Every day when he looked into the glass, and gave the last touch to his consummate toilette, he offered his grateful thanks to Providence that his family was not unworthy of him.

Benjamin Disraeli

Pride goes before, and shame follows after.

Proverb

Never underestimate a man who over-estimates himself.

Franklin D Roosevelt, on General Douglas MacArthur

He was like a cock who thought the sun had risen to hear him crow.

George Eliot

Pride is the mask of one's own faults.

Hebrew proverb

The truly proud man knows neither superiors nor inferiors. The first he does not admit of - the last he does not concern himself about.

William Hazlitt

PROBLEMS

The measure of success is not whether you have a tough problem to deal with, but whether it's the same problem you had last year.

If you're not part of the solution, you're part of the problem.

A problem well stated is a problem half solved.

If the only tool you have is a hammer, you tend to see every problem as a nail.

A problem is an opportunity in work clothes.

Problems are not stop signs, they are guidelines.

The greater the difficulty, the greater the glory.

Cicero

Work only on problems that are manifestly important and seem to be nearly impossible to resolve. That way, you will have a natural market for your product and no competition.

Edwin Land, founder of Polaroid

If you think the problem is bad now, just wait until we've solved it.

Arthur Kasspe

Problems are the price of progress. Don't bring me anything but trouble. Good news weakens me.

Charles F Kettering

PROFITS

It is a socialist idea that making profits is a vice; I consider the real vice is making losses.

Winston Churchill

A business that makes nothing but money is a poor business.

Henry Ford

When shallow critics denounce the profit motive inherent in our system of private enterprise they ignore the fact that it is an economic support of every human right we possess. Without it all rights would disappear.

Dwight D Eisenhower

Watch the costs and the profits will take care of themselves.

Andrew Carnegie

The smell of profit is clean and sweet, whatever the source.

Juvenal

Profits: money that has not been wasted.

Volume times zero isn't healthy.

Lee Iacocca

Every business has two financial objectives: one is to make money; the other, more elusive, is to make money consistently.

PROGRESS

The reasonable man adapts himself to the world; the unreasonable man persists in trying to adapt the world to himself. Therefore all progress depends on the unreasonable man.

George Bernard Shaw

The world is moving so fast these days that the man who says it can't be done is generally interrupted by someone doing it.

All progress is based upon a universal innate desire on the part of every organism to live beyond its income.

Samuel Butler

At every crossway on the road that leads to the future, each progressive spirit is opposed by a thousand men appointed to guard the past.

All progress grows out of discontent with things as they are: discomfort, disgust, displeasure, dissatisfaction, disease.

In human affairs, the best stimulus for running ahead is to have something we must run from.

p

Progress imposes not only new possibilities for the future but new restrictions

Is it progress if a cannibal uses knife and fork?

PROMISES

A man apt to promise is apt to forget.

Don't put it in my ear, but in my hand.
Russian proverb

He loses his thanks who promises and delays.
Latin proverb

A promise is binding in the inverse ratio of the numbers to whom it is made.

Vows made in storms are forgot in calm.
English proverb

We promise according to our hopes, and perform according to our fears.
La Rochefoucauld

Everyone's a millionaire where promises are concerned.

We promise much to avoid giving little.

An acre of performance is worth the whole Land of Promise.
James Howell

Half the promises people say were never kept, were never made.
Ed Howe

He who is the most slow in making a promise is the most faithful in the performance of it.
Rousseau

PROMOTION

If you work faithfully eight hours a day you may eventually get promoted high enough to work twelve hours a day.

You promote yourself every time you take on a new responsibility.

Comrades, you have lost a good captain to make him an ill general.

Montaigne

Mr Morgan buys his partners; I grow my own.

Andrew Carnegie

In a hierarchy, every employee tends to rise to his level of incompetence.

Laurence Peter

To blame a promotion that fails on the promoted person, as is usually done, is no more rational than to blame a capital investment that has gone sour on the money that was put into it.

Peter Drucker

I made myself almost too good as Number Two. So, in effect, what I had to do to get promoted was to get my boss promoted. Which I would advise anyone to do. That may sound cynical, but if you want to get ahead, promote your boss.

William George

PROPERTY

An acre in Middlesex is better than a principality in Utopia.

Macaulay

p

Thieves respect property. They merely wish the property to become their property that they may more perfectly respect it.

GK Chesterton

When the white man came, we had the land and they had the Bibles. Now they have the land and we have the Bibles.

Chief Dan George

Property is the fruit of labour; property is desirable; it is a positive good in the world. That someone should be rich shows that others may become rich, and hence, is just another encouragement to industry and enterprise.

Abraham Lincoln

Property: a bleach that takes stains out of character.

Our houses are such unwieldy property that we are often imprisoned rather than housed in them.

Thoreau

The dog is a lion in his own house.

Persian proverb

PRUDENCE

Prudence is a rich, ugly old maid courted by Incapacity.

William Blake

Call the bear "Uncle" till you are safe across the bridge.

Turkish proverb

No wise man stands behind an ass when he kicks.

A prudent man does not make the goat his gardener.

Hungarian proverb

He who wants a rose must respect the thorn.

Persian proverb

Measure a thousand times and cut once.

Turkish proverb

Caution, though often wasted, is a good risk to take.

Josh Billings

Caution is the eldest child of wisdom.

Victor Hugo

Drink nothing without seeing it, sign nothing without reading it.

Spanish proverb

Get out of the forest while you still have daylight.

Japanese proverb

PUBLISHING

There is some kind of notion abroad that because a book is humorous the publisher has to be funnier and madder than hell in marketing it.

SJ Perelman

No author is a man of genius to his publisher

Heinrich Heine

All a publisher has to do is write cheques at intervals, while a lot of deserving and industrious chappies rally round and do the real work.

PG Wodehouse

The relationship of an agent to a publisher is that of a knife to a throat.

Marvin Josephson

p

You cannot or at least should not try to argue with authors. Too many are like children whose tears can suddenly be changed to smiles if they are handled the right way.
  Michael Joseph, publisher

After being turned down by numerous publishers he decided to write for posterity.
  George Ade

Aren't we due a royalty statement?
  Prince Charles to his literary agent.

PUNCTUALITY

Punctuality is something that, if you have it, there's often no-one around to share it with you.

Punctuality is the virtue of the bored.

I've been on a calendar, but never on time.
  Marilyn Monroe

Punctuality: the art of guessing correctly how late the other party is going to be.

Punctuality is the politeness of kings.
  King Louis XVIII of France

Some people are always late, like the late King George V.
  Spike Milligan

Men count up the faults of those who keep them waiting.
  French proverb

The trouble with being punctual is that people think you have nothing more important to do.

If you're there before it's over, you're on time.
  James Walker

q

QUALITY

Quality is not an act. It is a habit.
Aristotle

Quality in a service or product is not what you put into it. It is what the client or customer gets out of it.
Peter Drucker

Quality is never an accident; it is always the result of intelligent effort.
John Ruskin

Conceal a flaw, and the world will imagine the worst.

Good quality is cheap; it's poor quality that is expensive.
Joe L Griffith

QUESTIONS

The "silly question" is the first intimation of some totally new development.

The uncreative mind can spot wrong answers, but it takes a creative mind to spot wrong questions.

He who asks is a fool for five minutes, but he who does not ask remains a fool forever.
Chinese proverb

Judge a man by his questions rather than by his answers.
Voltaire

Millions saw the apple fall but Newton was the one to ask why.

Better ask twice than lose your way once.
Danish proverb

To question a wise man is the beginning of wisdom.
German proverb

There aren't any embarrassing questions - just embarrassing answers.

REASON

Nothing has an uglier look to us than reason, when it is not on our side.

A man always has two reasons for doing anything - a good reason and the real reason.

JP Morgan

The man who listens to reason is lost: reason enslaves all those whose minds are not strong enough to master her.

George Bernard Shaw

We may take fancy for a companion, but follow reason as our guide.

Samuel Johnson

The last function of reason is to recognise that there are an infinity of things which surpass it.

Pascal

It is useless for us to attempt to reason a man out of a thing he has never been reasoned into.

Jonathan Swift

Error of opinion may be tolerated where reason is left free to combat it.

Thomas Jefferson

REPUTATION

Many a man's reputation would not know his character if they met on the street.

Elbert Hubbard

Do not worry about what people are thinking about you - for they are not thinking about you. They are wondering what you are thinking about them.

Reputation, reputation. O, I have lost my reputation. I have lost the immortal part, Sir, of myself, and what remains is bestial.

Shakespeare

The only time you realise you have a reputation is when you're not living up to it.

Jose Iturbi

It is easier to add to a good reputation than to get it.

Shall I be remembered after death? I sometimes think and hope so. But I trust I may not be found out before my death.

Samuel Butler

Reputation is often got without merit and lost without fault.

English proverb

How many "coming men" has one known! Where on earth do they all go to?

Sir Arthur Pinero

RESPONSIBILITY

Every man must carry his own sack to the mill.

Italian proverb

Everybody's business is nobody's business.

Responsibility is the price of greatness.

Winston Churchill

You can't escape the responsibility of tomorrow by evading it today.

Abraham Lincoln

That which is common to the greatest number has the least care bestowed upon it.

Aristotle

r

Unto whomsoever much is given, of him much shall be required.

Bible

No snowflake in an avalanche ever feels responsible.

A decision is what a man makes when he can't get anybody to serve on a committee.

Responsibility: a detachable burden easily shifted to the shoulders of God, Fate, Fortune, Luck, or one's neighbour. In the days of astrology it was customary to unload it upon a star.

Ambrose Bierce

The most anxious man in prison is the governor.

George Bernard Shaw

It is easy to dodge our responsibilities, but we cannot dodge the consequence of our responsibilities.

Lord Stamp

RETIREMENT

When a man retires and time is no longer a matter of urgent importance, his colleagues generally present him with a watch.

RC Sherriff

The problem with retirement is that you never know what day it is, what time it is, where you're supposed to be, or what you're supposed to be doing. It's a lot like working for the government.

Few men of action have been able to make a graceful exit at the appropriate time.

Malcolm Muggeridge

r

Two weeks is about the ideal length of time to retire.

Alex Comfort

The best time to start thinking about your retirement is before the boss does.

Retirement kills more people than hard work ever did.

Malcolm Forbes

When a man retires, his wife gets twice the husband, but only half the income.

Retirement from the concert world is like giving up smoking. You have got to finish completely.

Beniamino Gigli

Americans hardly ever retire from business: they are either carried out feet first or they jump from a window.

AL Goodheart

When you retire from the company you have to turn in your ulcers.

REVENGE

Revenge is a confession of pain.

Latin proverb

Revenge is a dish that should be eaten cold.

English proverb

In taking revenge, a man is but even with his enemy; but in passing it over, he is superior.

Francis Bacon

Revenge is a luscious fruit which you must leave to ripen.

Blood cannot be washed out with blood.

Persian proverb

Living well is the best revenge.

r

Nothing is more costly, nothing is more sterile, than vengeance.

Winston Churchill.

Revenge is often like biting a dog because the dog bit you.

A man that studieth revenge keeps his own wounds green.

Francis Bacon

Heat not a furnace for your foe so hot that it do singe thyself.

Shakespeare

RISK

A ship in harbour is safe, but that is not what ships are built for.

Behold the turtle. He makes progress only when he sticks his neck out.

Safe is risky.

Take calculated risks. That is quite different from being rash.

George S Patton

What would you attempt in life if you knew you could not fail?

Why not go out on a limb? Isn't that where the fruit is?

The desire for safety stands against every great and noble enterprise.

Tacitus

RULES

Hell, there are no rules here - we're trying to accomplish something.

Thomas Edison

Rules are for when brains run out.

Golden rule: he who has the gold makes the rules.

The golden rule is that there are no golden rules.

S

SCIENCE

The whole of science is nothing more than a refinement of everyday thinking.

Einstein

There is something fascinating about science. One gets such wholesale returns of conjecture out of such a trifling investment of fact.

George Bernard Shaw

Basic research is what I am doing when I don't know what I am doing.

Werner von Braun

My greatest discovery of all was the discovery of what people want to use.

Thomas Edison

Science has always promised two things not necessarily related - an increase first in our powers, second in our happiness and wisdom, and we have come to realise that it is the first and less important of the two promises which it has kept most abundantly.

Joseph Wood Krutch

The true scientist never loses the faculty of amazement. It is the essence of his being.

Hans Selye

A drug is a substance that when injected into a guinea pig produces a scientific paper.

SECURITY

The man who looks for security, even in the mind, is like a man who would chop off his limbs in order to have artificial ones which will give him no pain or trouble.

Henry Miller

The most beaten paths are certainly the surest; but do not hope to scare up much game on them.

André Gide

Some of the most insecure things in the world are called "securities".

The protected man doesn't need luck; therefore it seldom visits him.

Alan Harrington

People wish to be settled; only as far as they are unsettled is there any hope for them.

Ralph Waldo Emerson

The physic task which a person can and must do for himself is not to feel secure but to be able to tolerate insecurity.

Erich Fromm

SELLING

Sell the sizzle, not the steak.

A man without a smiling face must not open a shop.

Chinese proverb

Sales resistance is the triumph of mind over patter.

If you want to buy from us we speak English, but if you want to sell to us you must speak German.

Helmut Kohl

Don't oversell. If you do, it's like knocking on a turtle shell trying to get him to stick his head out.

Don't sell me books, sell me knowledge.

Don't sell me insurance, sell me peace of mind and a secure future for my family. Don't sell me clothes, sell me style, attractiveness and a sharper image. Don't sell me a house, sell me comfort and pride in ownership.

Who will sell a blind horse praises the feet.

German proverb

The fish sees the bait, not the hook.

Chinese proverb

"Don't you know that you can't sell insurance without a licence?"
"I knew I wasn't selling any but I didn't know the reason."

He's a very independent salesman - he takes orders from nobody.

An ideal salesman has the curiosity of a cat, the tenacity of a bulldog, the friendship of a little child, the diplomacy of a wayward husband, the patience of a self-sacrificing wife, the enthusiasm of a Sinatra fan, the assurance of a Harvard man, the good humour of a comedian, the simplicity of a jackass, and the tireless energy of a bill collector.

Harry G Moock

I stand behind every car I sell. I help push it.

The sales manager stood before the progress chart which indicated the sales of each representative with coloured pins. "Smith", he said, "I'm not going to fire you, but just to emphasise the insecurity of your position I'm loosening the pin a little."

Top salesman: a live wire with good connections.

First salesman: "I made some very valuable contacts today".
Second salesman: "I didn't get any orders either".

I used to sell furniture for a living. The trouble was, it was my own.

Les Dawson

Auctioneer: a man who proclaims with a hammer that he has picked a pocket with his tongue.

Ambrose Bierce

SEX

If it wasn't for pickpockets and frisking at airports I wouldn't have any sex life at all.

Rodney Dangerfield

A man who marries his mistress creates a vacancy in the position.

James Goldsmith

It's so long since I've had sex I've forgotten who ties up whom.

Joan Rivers

Ten men waiting for me at the door? Send one of them home, I'm tired.

Mae West

Basically, I wanted a woman who was an economist in the kitchen and a whore in bed. I wound up with a woman who was a whore in the kitchen and an economist in bed.

Geoffrey Gorer

What part of "no" don't you understand?

Rita Rudner

Sex - the poor man's polo.

A promiscuous person is someone who is getting more sex than you are.

Victor Lownes

I'm such a good lover because I practise a lot on my own.

Woody Allen

Man cannot live by bed alone.

I don't see so much of Alfred any more since he got so interested in sex.

Mrs Alfred Kinsey

It doesn't matter what you do in the bedroom as long as you don't do it in the streets and frighten the horses.

Mrs Patrick Campbell

He said it was artificial respiration, but now I find that I am to have his child.

I am always looking for meaningful one-night stands.

Dudley Moore

SILENCE

Keep quiet and people will think you are a philosopher.

Latin proverb

Silence is the most perfect expression of scorn.

George Bernard Shaw

Silence is one of the hardest arguments to refute.

GK Chesterton

Better to remain silent and be thought a fool, than to speak out and remove all doubt.

Abraham Lincoln

Silence is also speech.

Yiddish proverb

The silent dog is the first to bite.

German proverb

In human intercourse the tragedy begins, not when there is misunderstanding about words, but when silence is not understood.

Thoreau

That man's silence is wonderful to listen to.

Thomas Hardy

The most silent people are generally those who think most highly of themselves.

William Hazlitt

Most of us know how to say nothing. Few of us know when.

A man is known by the silence he keeps.

SIMPLICITY

Less is more.

Robert Browning

The ability to simplify means to eliminate the unnecessary so that the necessary may speak.

Hans Hoffmann

Simplicity is the mean between ostentation and rusticity.

Alexander Pope

Affected simplicity is an elegant imposture.

La Rochefoucauld

It is proof of high culture to say the greatest matters in the simplest way.

Ralph Waldo Emerson

Simplicity is the most deceitful mistress that ever betrayed man.

Henry Adams

Simplicity of character is the natural result of profound thought.

William Hazlitt

He was a simple soul who had not been introduced to his own subconscious.

Warwick Deeping

SINCERITY

People are always sincere. They change sincerities, that's all.

Tristan Bernard

I am not sincere, even when I am saying that I am not sincere.

Jules Renard

It's never what you say, but how you make it sound sincere.

Marya Mannes

A little sincerity is a dangerous thing and a great deal of it is absolutely fatal.

Oscar Wilde

Weak people cannot be sincere.

La Rochefoucauld

To stupid people sincerity is one continuous process of self-sacrifice.

The most exhausting thing in life, I have discovered, is being insincere.

Anne Morrow Lindbergh

SIZE

Size isn't everything. The whale is endangered, while the ant continues to do just fine.

Bill Vaughan

If you think you're too small to have an impact, try going to bed with a mosquito in your room.

Anita Roddick

Great engines turn on small pivots.

English proverb

Any intelligent fool can make things bigger, more complex, and more violent. It takes a touch of genius - and a lot of courage - to move in the opposite direction.

EF Schumacher

If you can build a business up big enough, it's respectable.

Will Rogers

The dinosaur's eloquent lesson is that if some bigness is good, an overabundance of bigness is not necessarily better.

Eric Johnston

A big corporation is more or less blamed for being big; it is only big if it gives service. If it doesn't give service, it gets small faster than it grew big.

William Knudsen

SLANDER

A slander is like a hornet; if you cannot kill it dead the first blow, better not strike at it.

HW Shaw

If slander be a snake, it is a winged one - it flies as well as creeps.

Douglas Jerrold

People are more slanderous from vanity than from malice.

La Rochefoucauld

Folk whose own behaviour is most ridiculous are always to the fore in slandering others.

Molière

Slander, like coal, will either dirty your hand or burn it.

Russian proverb

It takes your enemy and your friend, working together, to hurt you to the heart; the one to slander you and the other to get the news to you.

Mark Twain

Have patience awhile; slanders are not long-lived. Truth is the child of time; ere long she shall appear to vindicate thee.

Immanuel Kant

The more implausible a slander is, the better fools remember it.

SLEEP

The amount of sleep required by the average person is just five minutes more.

A man is not always asleep when his eyes are shut.

Sleeping at the wheel is a good way to keep from growing old.

Sleep is the best cure for waking troubles.

Spanish proverb

Sleep: the poor man's wealth.

Laugh and the world laughs with you, snore and you sleep alone.

Anthony Burgess

That we are not much sicker and much madder than we are is due exclusively to that most blessed and blessing of all natural graces, sleep.

Aldous Huxley

The best thing about lying in bed late is that you learn to distinguish between first things and trivia, for whatever presses on you has to prove its importance before it makes you move.

Max Lerner

There will be sleeping enough in the grave.

Irish proverb

SMOKING

As ye smoke, so shall ye reek.

Tobacco: the Indians' revenge.

The best cigarette filter is the cellophane on an unwrapped package.

I kissed my first woman and smoked my first cigarette on the same day; I have never had time for tobacco since.

Arturo Toscanini

To the average smoker the world is his ashtray.

Alexander Chase

I have every sympathy with the American who was so horrified by what he had read about the effects of smoking that he gave up reading.

Henry G Strauss

Perfection is such a nuisance that I often regret having cured myself of using tobacco.

Emile Zola

Smoking is very bad for you and should only be done because it looks so good. People who don't smoke have a terrible time finding something polite to do with their lips.

PJ O'Rourke

SNOBBERY

A fine imitation of self-esteem for those who can't afford the real thing.

Frederick Morton

Laughter would be bereaved if snobbery died.

Peter Ustinov

Yeats is becoming so aristocratic, he's evicting imaginary tenants.

Oliver St John Gogarty

The true snob never rests; there is always a higher goal to attain, and there are, by the same token, always more and more people to look down upon.

Russell Lynes

All think their little set mankind.

Hannah More

An uppish class sometimes mistakes itself for an upper class.

Snobbery is the pride of those who are not sure of their position.

The superiority of some men is merely local. They are great because their associates are little.

Samuel Johnson

Snobs talk as if they had begotten their own ancestors.

Herbert Agar

SPEECH
(Opening)

Thank you for the generous introduction. After that I can hardly wait to hear what I have to say.

Coming here today, my wife offered me some sage advice. "Don't try to be charming, witty, or intellectual. Just be yourself."

Sometimes I feel like Groucho Marx, who said: "Before I speak I have something important to say".

I hope that when I've finished speaking, I don't experience what Adlai Stevenson did the time he spoke at a small college. When the speech was over, a young man approached him and said: "Mr Stevenson, that was a wonderful speech - absolutely superfluous". Stevenson was taken aback but graciously replied: "Thank you. I'm glad you liked it. I intend to have it published posthumously." The student replied: "Great. The sooner the better".

The last time our chairman introduced me and was told to be brief, he began: "The less said about William Davis, the better...."

Speaking to you today, I'm violating one of the three pieces of immortal advice from Winston Churchill, who said: "Never try to walk up a wall that's leaning towards you. Never try to kiss a person that's leaning away from you. And never speak to a group that knows more about the subject than you do".

S

A toastmaster once advised me that an after-dinner speech should always be short. He said:
Be accurate!
Be brief!
And then be seated!

Ladies and gentlemen, I promise you that I shall be as brief as possible - no matter how long it takes me.

Thank you for that marvellous obituary.

I'm so confident tonight, I didn't even wear my best suit.

I once heard a chairman say: Mr Jones will now give his address. Mr Jones got up and said: 339 Park Avenue. And sat down again.

Your chairman just said to me: "Would you like to speak now or shall we let them go on enjoying themselves for a little longer?".

At your reception earlier someone said to me: "Oh, I have heard so much about you, now I'd like to hear your side of the story".

For those of you who have had a heavy day I've booked an alarm call for the end of my speech.

Your chairman asked if I believed in free speech. I said of course I did - it's fundamental to our democracy. He said: "Good, can you make one next week?".

Friends. Well, I feel I know you too well to call you ladies and gentlemen.

S

I'm sorry I am late. The lift said "Six people only". So I had to wait for five more.

I'm the only one on the top table I have never heard of.

It's a change to find my name in bigger type than the soup.

I'm not a proud speaker. If you don't wish to applaud I'll settle for enthusiastic nods.

You will be relieved to hear that I do not intend to use the full two hours allotted to me.

Heckle Stoppers
I shall have to ask your mother to take you home.

Any more cracks like that and your wife and I are through.

I'd like to help you out - tell me, which way did you come in?

What exactly is on your mind? If you'll excuse the exaggeration?

If I want you, I'll rattle your cage.

Were you there for the fitting of that suit?

You seem happy tonight. No school tomorrow?

Must be a full moon tonight.

He must be a bundle of fun at home.

STUPIDITY

When a finger points at the moon, the imbecile looks at the finger.
Chinese proverb

He that hath a head of wax must not walk in the sun.
English proverb

He that makes himself an ass must not take it ill if men ride him.

Thomas Fuller

It is so pleasant to come across people more stupid than ourselves. We love them at once for being so.

Jerome K Jerome

Whenever a man does a stupid thing it is always from the noblest motive.

Oscar Wilde

Better an empty purse than an empty head.

German proverb

Nothing in all the world is more dangerous than sincere ignorance and conscientious stupidity.

Martin Luther King Jr

What makes stupidity really insufferable is that it is forever in action - ignorance knows no rest.

STYLE

Style is when they're running you out of town and you make it look like you're leading a parade.

William Battie

Style is a magic wand, and turns everything to gold that it touches.

Logan Pearsall Smith

In matters of grave importance, style, not sincerity, is the vital thing.

Oscar Wilde

The only real elegance is in the mind; if you've got that, the rest really comes from it.

Diana Vreeland

Style is the dress of thoughts.

Lord Chesterfield

SUCCESS

To succeed, jump as quickly at opportunities as you do at conclusions.

Benjamin Franklin

For every person who climbs the ladder of success there are a dozen waiting for the elevator.

Success is a great deodorant.

Secrets for success:
1. Get up Early.
2. Work Hard.
3. Strike Oil.

Eighty per cent of success is showing up.

Woody Allen

You'll die if you sit on your laurels.

Success is a journey, not a destination.

Everybody loves success, but they hate successful people.

John McEnroe

Success gives some people big heads and others big headaches.

Success has many friends.

Greek proverb

A successful man is one who makes more money than his wife can spend. A successful woman is one who can find such a man.

Lana Turner

Success has ruined many a man.

Benjamin Franklin

Every man who is high up loves to think that he has done it all himself; and the wife smiles and lets it go at that.

JM Barrie

The common idea that success spoils people by making them vain, egotistic, and self-complacent is erroneous; on the contrary, it makes them, for the most part, humble, tolerant and kind. Failure makes people cruel and bitter.

Somerset Maugham

There is always something about success that displeases even your best friends.

Oscar Wilde

All you need in this life is ignorance and confidence, and then success is sure.

Mark Twain

Success is the ability to get along with some people and ahead of others.

Successful people are the ones who can think up things for the rest of the world to keep busy at.

One of the great advantages of success lies in the fact that you don't have to listen to good advice any more.

Success: when a man stops keeping track of the money and starts counting calories.

The only place where success comes before work is in the dictionary.

The penalty of success is to be bored by the people who used to snub you.

Nancy Astor

There's no secret about success. Did you ever know a successful man that didn't tell you about it?

The toughest thing about success is that you've got to keep on being a success. Talent is only a starting point in business. You've got to keep working that talent.

Irving Berlin

S

My rise to the top was through sheer ability - and inheritance.

Malcolm Forbes

The compensation of a very early success is a conviction that life is a romantic matter. In the best sense one stays young.

F Scott Fitzgerald

Unless a man has been taught what to do with success after getting it, the achievement of it must inevitably leave him prey to boredom.

Bertrand Russell

TALK

Don't talk about yourself; it will be done when you leave.

Addison Mitzner

Talk is cheap.

English proverb

The secret of being tiresome is in telling everything.

Voltaire

Some people would say more if they talked less.

I don't like people to talk while I'm interrupting.

Another of life's problems is how to keep ignorant people from talking.

Some people talk simply because they think sound is more manageable than silence.

The voice is a second face.

Little said is soon amended.

Cervantes

Talk does not cook rice.

Chinese proverb

People do not seem to talk for the sake of expressing their opinions, but to maintain an opinion for the sake of talking.

William Hazlitt

Many people would be more truthful were it not for their uncontrollable desire to talk.

Edgar Watson Howe

The tongue is more to be feared than the sword.

Japanese proverb

We talk little when vanity does not make us.

La Rochefoucauld

What is uttered is finished and done with.

Thomas Mann

The unluckiest insolvent in the world is the man whose expenditure of speech is too great for his income of ideas.

Christopher Morley

They always talk who never think.

Matthew Prior

No man would listen to you talk if he didn't know it was his turn next.

Edgar Watson Howe

At a dinner party one should eat wisely but not too well, and talk well but not too wisely.

Somerset Maugham

How time flies when you are doing all the talking.

TAXES

Everybody should pay his income tax with a smile. I tried it, but they wanted cash.

Next to being shot at and missed, there is nothing quite as satisfying as a tax refund.

Taxes are the way the government has of artificially inducing the rainy day everybody has been saving for.

Taxation is the art of so plucking the goose as to obtain the largest amount of feathers with the least amount of hissing.

A government which robs Peter to pay Paul can always rely on the support of Paul.

George Bernard Shaw

This is the season of the year when we discover that we owe most of our success to Uncle Sam!

Wall Street Journal

It is the part of a good shepherd to fleece his flock, not to flay it.

Tiberius

A toast to the Inland Revenue. You really have to hand it to those boys.

Inland Revenue: the world's most successful mail order business.

The taxpayer - that's someone who works for the federal government but doesn't have to take a civil service exam.

Ronald Reagan

Income tax has made more liars out of the American people than golf.

Will Rogers

Income tax returns are the most imaginative fiction being written today.

Herman Wouk

Don't get too excited about a tax cut. It's like a mugger giving you back fare for a taxi.

All money nowadays seems to be produced with a natural homing instinct for the Treasury.

There is one difference between a tax collector and a taxidermist - the taxidermist leaves the hide.

The point to remember is that what the government gives it must first take away.

TEAMWORK

No member of a crew is praised for the rugged individuality of his rowing.

Ralph Waldo Emerson

It takes two wings for a bird to fly.

It is better to have one person working with you than having three people working for you.

Dwight D Eisenhower

As the mouse said to the elephant as they walked across a bridge: "together we're shaking this thing".

A single arrow is easily broken, but not ten in a bundle.

Japanese proverb

THRIFT

It's very well to be thrifty, but don't amass a hoard of regrets.

A penny saved is a penny earned.

A penny saved is a penny to squander.

Ambrose Bierce

A man often pays dear for a small frugality.

Ralph Waldo Emerson

Anyone who lives within his means suffers from a lack of imagination.

Lionel Stander

Save water, shower with a friend.

Slogan in the 1970s

He that considers in prosperity will be less afflicted in adversity.

Economy is too late at the bottom of the purse.

There is no profit in going to bed early to save candles if the result is twins.

The secret is to live as cheaply the first few days after payday as you lived the last few days before.

The petty economies of the rich are just as amazing as the silly extravagances of the poor.
William Feather

TIME

People who make the worst use of their time are the same ones who complain that there is never enough time.

Time is money, especially overtime.

You can't make footprints in the sands of time by sitting down.

Time gives good advice.
Maltese proverb

Time is the most valuable thing a man can spend.

Until you value yourself, you will not value time. Until you value your time, you will not do anything with it.

You will never find time for anything. If you want time you must make it.

A man who has taken your time recognises no debt; yet it is the one he can never repay.
Seneca

Counting time is not so important as making time count.

Time and tide wait for no man.
English proverb

Better late than never.

Time is money, and many people pay their debts with it.

Time is a dressmaker specialising in alterations.

Time and I against any two.
Spanish proverb

Why kill time when you can employ it?

Time wounds all heels.

I·haven't the time to take my time.

Time makes more converts than reason.

Time, which changes people, does not alter the image we have retained of them.
Marcel Proust

TOASTS

May you live as long as you want, and not want as long as you live.

May the Lord love us but not call us too soon.

Let us toast the fools. But for them the rest of us could not succeed.
Mark Twain

Love to one, friendship to many, and goodwill to all.

May we be happy and our enemies know it.

May you have warmth in your igloo, oil in your lamp, and peace in your heart.
Eskimo toast

May the roof above us never fall in, and may we friends gathered below never fall out.

May your fire never go out.

May your well never run dry.

Here's to becoming top banana without losing touch with the bunch.
Bill Copeland, on a promotion

May friendship, like wine, improve as time advances, and may we always have old wines, old friends, and young cares.

When there's snow on the roof, there's fire in the furnace.

Toast to maturity

To the Great Unknown - who is waiting to do us a favour.

May you live to a hundred years with one extra year to repent.

A health to you,
A wealth to you,
And the best that life can give to you.
May fortune still be kind to you.
And happiness be true to you,
And life be long and good to you,
Is the toast of all your friends to you.

Here's to Eternity - may we spend it in as good company as this night finds us.

To your good health, old friend, may you live for a thousand years, and I be there to count them.

TRAVEL

Flying first class is a bit like being in a hospital - they wake you up every few hours to give you orange juice.

The hotel was so up-market that even room service was ex-directory.

There are two classes of travel - first class, and with children.

Robert Benchley

It is easier to find a travel companion than to get rid of one.

Art Buchwald

t

To give you an idea of how fast we travelled: we left Spokane with two rabbits and when we got to Topeka, we still had only two.

Bob Hope

They say travel broadens the mind; but you must have the mind.

GK Chesterton

At my age travel broadens the behind.

Stephen Fry

Always choose the oldest customs official. No chance of promotion.

Somerset Maugham

Travel teaches toleration.

Disraeli

Fly first class - or your heirs will.

The heaviest baggage for a traveller is an empty purse.

English proverb

Hawaii has the same weather all year round. Wonder how their conversations start?

Everybody in fifteenth-century Spain was wrong about where China was and as a result, Columbus discovered Caribbean vacations.

PJ O'Rourke

On a Polar expedition begin with a clear idea which Pole you are aiming at, and try to start facing the right way. Choose your companions carefully - you may have to eat them.

WC Sellar

Every year it takes less time to fly across the Atlantic and more time to drive to the office.

Drive carefully! Remember it's not only a car that can be recalled by its maker.

Like all great travellers, I have seen more than I remember, and remember more than I have seen.

Disraeli

It used to be a good hotel, but that proves nothing - I used to be a good boy.

Mark Twain

TROUBLE

Why hoard your troubles? They have no market value, so just throw them away.

Never trouble trouble till trouble troubles you.

The best place to put your troubles is in your pocket - the one with a hole in it.

He that seeks trouble always finds it.

English proverb

I am an old man and have known a great many troubles, but most of them never happened.

Problems are the price of progress. Don't bring me anything but trouble. Progress weakens me.

Trouble is the structural steel that goes into the building of character.

Golf without bunkers and hazards would be tame and monotonous. So would life.

A problem well stated is a problem half solved.

The greater the difficulty, the greater the glory.

Cicero

Problems are not stop signs, they are guidelines.

The trouble with trouble is that it always starts out like fun.

TRUTH

Baldwin occasionally stumbles over the truth, but he always hastily picks himself up and hurries on as if nothing had happened.
Winston Churchill

Truth for him was a moving target; he never aimed for the bull's eye and rarely pierced the outer ring.
Hugh Cudlipp

If you speak the truth have a foot in the stirrup.
Turkish proverb

It is always the best policy to speak the truth, unless of course, you are an exceptionally good liar.
Jerome K Jerome

What is true by lamplight is not always true by sunlight.
Joubert

Tell the truth, and so puzzle and confound your adversaries.
Sir Henry Wotton

It is the customary fate of new truths to begin as heresies and to end as superstitions.
TH Huxley

Truth needs no memory.

Platitudes are among the most useful things in the world for those who know how to use them, for truth is not the worse for being obvious, undeniable, or familiar.

It is hard to believe that a man is telling the truth when you know that you would lie if you were in his place.
HL Mencken

The truth would become more popular if it were not always stating ugly facts.

In this world, truth can wait;
she's used to it.
Douglas Jerrold

If it is not true it is very well
invented.

I have too much respect for
the truth to drag it out on
every trifling occasion.
Mark Twain

Something unpleasant is
coming when men are
anxious to tell the truth.
Benjamin Disraeli

Never tell a story because it
is true: tell it because it is a
good story.
John Pentland Manhaffy

Truth is a rare and precious
commodity. We must be
sparing in its use.
CP Scott

Some men love truth so
much that they seem to be
in continual fear lest she
should catch a cold on over-
exposure.
Samuel Butler

UNDERSTANDING

It is better to understand little than to misunderstand a lot.

Anatole France

God grant me to contend with those that understand me.

Thomas Fuller

Men are most apt to believe what they least understand.

Montaigne

He who does not understand your silence will probably not understand your words.

Elbert Hubbard

Understanding is the beginning of approving.

Each of us really understands in others only those feelings he is capable of producing himself.

André Gide

To understand everything makes one very indulgent.

Madame de Staël

Much learning does not teach understanding.

Heraclitus

UNITY

Weak things united become strong.

We must all hang together, or assuredly we shall all hang separately.

Benjamin Franklin

By union the smallest states thrive, by discord the greatest are destroyed.

Sallust

If a link is broken, the whole chain breaks.

Yiddish proverb

All for one; one for all.

Dumas, The Three Musketeers

There are only two forces that unite men - fear and interest.

Napoleon Bonaparte

It is always possible to bind together a considerable number of people in love, so long as there are other people left over to receive the manifestations of their aggressiveness.

Sigmund Freud

UNIVERSITY

If you feel that you have both feet planted on level ground then the university has failed you.

Robert Goheen

It (Oxford) is a sanctuary in which exploded systems and obsolete prejudices find shelter and protection after they have been hunted out of every corner of the world.

Adam Smith

What poor education I have received has been gained in the University of Life.

Horatio Bottomley

I was a modest, good-humoured boy. It is Oxford that has made me insufferable.

Max Beerbohm

A man who has never gone to school may steal from a freight car; but if he has a university education, he may steal the whole railroad.

Theodore Roosevelt

I cannot see that lectures can do so much good as reading the books from which the lectures are taken.

Samuel Johnson

A professor is one who talks in someone else's sleep.

WH Auden

VALUE

You don't get paid for the hour. You get paid for the value you bring to an hour.

What you really value is what you miss, not what you have.

Jorge Luis Borges

That which costs little is less valued.

Cervantes

We never know the worth of water till the well is dry.

Thomas Fuller

Everybody in the world is good for something. At least they can be a bad example.

There is no such thing as absolute value in this world. You can only estimate what a thing is worth to *you*.

What we must decide is perhaps how we are valuable rather than how valuable we are.

Edgar Friedenberg

VISION

Vision is the art of seeing things invisible.

Jonathan Swift

Every man takes the limits of his own field of vision for the limits of the world.

Schopenhauer

The vision must be followed by the venture. It is not enough to stare up the steps. We must step up the stairs.

Vance Hepner

The most pathetic person in the world is someone who has sight but no vision.

Helen Keller

Some things have to be believed to be seen.

WEALTH

If you can actually count your money, then you're not rich.

J Paul Getty

The way to wealth is as plain as the way to market.

Benjamin Franklin

You may try to destroy wealth and find that all you have done is increase poverty.

Winston Churchill

A rich man is nothing but a poor man with money.

WC Fields

Wealth can't buy health, but health can buy wealth.

Thoreau

Wealth is not his that has it, but his that enjoys it.

I've been rich and I've been poor. Rich is better.

Sophie Tucker

I am opposed to millionaires, but it would be dangerous to offer me the position.

Mark Twain

He has not acquired a fortune; the fortune has acquired him.

Prosperity is only an instrument to be used; not a deity to be worshipped.

Calvin Coolidge

The brother had rather see the sister rich than make her so.

Heiresses are never jilted.

Poverty is an anomaly to rich people. It is very difficult to make out why people who want dinner do not ring the bell.

Walter Bagehot

The wretchedness of being rich is that you live with rich people.

Logan Pearsall Smith

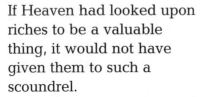

If Heaven had looked upon riches to be a valuable thing, it would not have given them to such a scoundrel.

Jonathan Swift

Don't make fun of the rich. You may be rich some day yourself.

The larger a man's roof, the more snow it collects.

Persian proverb

This is the posture of fortune's slave: one foot in the gravy, one foot in the grave.

James Thurber

I wish that dear Karl could have spent some time acquiring capital instead of merely writing about it.

Jenny Marx

No woman can be too rich or too thin.

Duchess of Windsor

There's no reason to be the richest man in the cemetery. You can't do business from there.

Colonel Sanders

WINNING

Winning is a habit. Unfortunately, so is losing.

If it doesn't matter who wins, then how come they keep score?

Anyone can win - unless there happens to be a second entry.

Winning isn't everything, but the will to win is everything.

Whoever said "It's not whether you win or lost that counts", probably lost.

Another victory like that and we are done for.

Pyrrhus

Remember, it doesn't matter whether you win or lose; what matters is whether I win or lose.

Darrin Weinberg

One should always play fairly when one has the winning cards.

Oscar Wilde

WISDOM

Wisdom rises upon the ruins of folly.

Thomas Fuller

He is no wise man that cannot play the fool upon occasion.

How prone to doubt, how cautious are the wise!

Homer

It is very foolish to wish to be exclusively wise.

It is easier to be wise on behalf of others than to be so for ourselves.

Nine-tenths of wisdom is to be wise in time.

Theodore Roosevelt

Youth is the time to study wisdom; old age is the time to practise it.

Rousseau

It is characteristic of wisdom not to do desperate things.

Thoreau

It takes a wise man to recognise a wise man.

He swallowed a lot of wisdom, but it seemed as if all of it had gone down the wrong way.

The farther he went west, the more convinced he felt that the wise men came from the east.

Sydney Smith

Not by years but by disposition is wisdom acquired.

Plautus

Be wiser than other people, if you can, but do not tell them so.

Lord Chesterfield

Many persons might have attained to wisdom had they not assumed that they already possessed it.

Seneca

Knowledge comes but wisdom lingers.

Tennyson

Some are wise, some are otherwise.

WIT

Wit is the power to say what everybody would like to have said, if they had happened to think of it.

Whistler

The greatest fault of penetrating wit is to go beyond the mark.

La Rochefoucauld

Wit has truth in it: wisecracking is simply calisthenics with words.

Dorothy Parker

A man must have a good share of wit himself to endure a great share in another.

Lord Chesterfield

Even wit is a burden if it talks too long.

Latin proverb

Wit is far more often a shield than a lance.

An original wit is a guy who has heard the gag before you do.

Wit ought to be a glorious treat, like caviar: never spread it about like marmalade.

Noël Coward

An ounce of wit is worth a pound of sorrow.

Sharp wits, like sharp knives, do often cut their owners' fingers.

Arrowsmith

Wit in conversation is, in the midwives' phrase, a quick conception and an easy delivery.

Jonathan Swift

Impropriety is the soul of wit.

Somerset Maugham

Wit is the salt of conversation, not the food.

William Hazlitt

WORK

Work is something that when we have it, we wish we didn't, and when we don't have it, we wish we did.

There are many formulas for success - but none of them work unless you do.

He that wishes to eat the nut does not mind cracking the shell.

Polish proverb

When it comes to work, there are many who will stop at nothing.

Work is the easiest activity man has invented to escape boredom.

Choose a job you love, and you will never have to work a day in your life.

Confucius

W

The man who rolls up his shirt sleeves is rarely in danger of losing his shirt.

Work expands so as to fill the time available for its completion.

C Northcote Parkinson

Being busy does not always mean real work. The object of all work is production or accomplishment and to either of these ends there must be forethought, system, planning, intelligence, and honest purpose as well as perspiration. Seeming to do is not doing.

Thomas Edison

Nobody ever drowned in his own sweat.

Work is so much more fun than fun.

Trammell Crow

The first five days of the week are when you work to keep up with the competition. It's on Saturdays and Sundays that you get ahead of them.

Curt Carlson

My grandfather once told me that there were two kinds of people: those who do the work and those who take the credit. He told me to try to be in the first group; there was much less competition.

Indira Gandhi

It's always been and always will be the same in the world: the horse does the work and the coachman is tipped.

One chops the wood, the other does the grunting.

Yiddish proverb

Work is the curse of the drinking classes.

Oscar Wilde

I like work; it fascinates me. I can sit and look at it for hours.
Jerome K Jerome

Employee: "There's no point in working late to impress management. They all go home early".

Never itch for anything you aren't willing to scratch for.

Don't tell me how hard you work. Tell me how much you get done.
James Ling

When your work speaks for itself, don't interrupt.
Henry Kaiser

If hard work were such a wonderful thing, surely the rich would have kept it all to themselves.

Hard work never killed anybody, but why take a chance on being the first?

Why do men delight in work? Fundamentally, I suppose, because there is a sense of relief and pleasure in getting something done - a kind of satisfaction not unlike that which a hen enjoys on laying an egg.
HL Mencken

Work is the refuge of people who have nothing better to do.
Oscar Wilde

Robinson Crusoe started the forty-hour week. He had all his work done by Friday.

Nothing is really work unless you would rather be doing something else.
Sir James Barrie

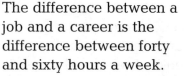

The difference between a job and a career is the difference between forty and sixty hours a week.

Robert Frost

I am a friend of the working man, and I would rather be a friend than be one.

Clarence Darrow

WORRY

Worry is the interest paid on trouble before it falls due.

An activity as useless as whispering in a boiler factory.

If you want to test your memory, try to remember what you were worrying about one year ago today.

Wear your worries like a loose garment.

If you must worry, don't worry out loud. It wastes the time of others as well as your own.

Keep cool: it will be all one a hundred years hence.

Ralph Waldo Emerson

The longer we dwell on our misfortunes the greater is their power to harm us.

Voltaire

It is not work that kills men; it is worry. Worry is rust upon the blade.

Henry Ward Beecher

Z

ZEAL

What wins out when ability falters.

Zeal without knowledge is fire without light.
Thomas Fuller

Let a man in a garret but burn with intensity and he will set fire to the world.

Authors quoted in this book include -

Allen, Woody (1935 -). American film actor, writer, and director.

Atkinson, Brooks (1894-1984). American drama critic and essayist.

Barrie, JM (1860-1937). Scottish dramatist and novelist.

Baruch, Bernard (1870-1965). American businessman and statesman.

Beecham, Sir Thomas (1879-1961). English conductor.

Beerbohm, Sir Max (1872-1956). English essayist and caricaturist.

Bierce, Ambrose (1842-1914). American journalist, short-story writer, poet.

Billings, Josh (1818-1885). American humorist

Byron, Lord (1788-1824). English poet

Carnegie, Dale (1888-1955). American author and lecturer.

Carroll, Lewis. Pen name of Charles Lutwidge Dodson (1832-1898). English writer and mathematician.

Cervantes, Miguel de (1547-1616). Spanish novelist, dramatist, poet.

Chesterfield, Lord (1694-1773). English statesman and man of letters.

Chesterton, GK (1874-1936). English journalist, essayist, novelist, poet.

Colton, Charles Caleb (1780-1832). English writer and clergyman.

Coward, Noël (1899-1973). English playwright, actor, composer.

Disraeli, Benjamin (1804-1881). English statesman and novelist.

Dostoevsky, Fyodor (1821-1881) Russian writer.

Edison, Thomas Alva (1847-1931). American inventor.

Einstein, Albert (1879-1955). German-Swiss-American physicist.

Emerson, Ralph Waldo (1803-1882). American poet, essayist, philosopher.

Fields, WC (1880-1946). American humorist.

Franklin, Benjamin (1706-1790). American statesman, writer, inventor, printer, scientist.

Gide, André (1869-1951). French novelist, essayist, critic, editor, translator.

Goethe, Johann Wolfgang von (1749-1832). German poet, playwright, novelist.

Goldwyn, Sam (1882-1974). Polish-born American film producer.

Hammarskjöld, Dag (1905-1961). Swedish statesman, secretary-general of the United Nations.

Hazlitt, William (1778-1830). English essayist and critic.

Heine, Heinrich (1797-1856) German poet, satirist, journalist.

Heraclitus (c 500 BC). Greek philosopher.

Hoffer, Eric (1902-1983). American philosopher and author.

Howe, Edgar Watson (1853-1937). American editor, author, essayist.

Hubbard, Elbert (1856-1915). American businessman, writer, printer.

Huxley, Thomas Henry (1825-1895). English biologist, teacher, writer.

Jefferson, Thomas (1743-1826). American statesman, third president of the United States.

Jerome, Jerome K (1859-1927). English novelist and playwright.

Jerrold, Douglas (1803-1857). English playwright and humorist.

Johnson, Samuel (1709-1784). English lexicographer, essayist, poet, wit.

Kant, Immanuel (1724-1804). German philosopher.

Krutch, Joseph Wood (1893-1970). American essayist, critic, teacher.

La Rochefoucauld, François, Duc de (1613-1680). French writer.

Lippmann, Walter (1889-1974). American newspaper columnist and author.

Macaulay, Thomas Babington, 1st Baron Macaulay (1800-1859). English statesman, poet, historian, biographer.

Marquis, Donald (1878-1937). American newspaperman and humorist.

Martial - full name Marcus Valerius Martialis (AD 42-102). Latin poet born in Spain.

Maugham, Somerset (1874-1965). English novelist and playwright.

Mencken, HL (1880-1956). American newspaperman, editor, writer.

Montaigne, Michel (1533-1592). French moralist and essayist.

Nietzsche, Friedrich (1844-1900). German philosopher.

Parker, Dorothy (1893-1967). American writer of short stories, verse, criticism.

Parkinson, C Northcote (1909-1993). American historian and writer.

Perelman, SJ (1904-1979). American humorist.

Plautus - full name Titus Maccius Plautus (254-184 BC). Roman comic playwright.

Rogers, Will (1879-1935). American actor and humorist.

Russell, Bertrand, 3rd Earl Russell (1872-1970). English philosopher, mathematician, social reformer.

Santayana, George (1863-1952). Spanish-born American philosopher, poet, novelist, critic.

Schopenhauer, Arthur (1788-1860). German philosopher.

Seneca - full name Lucius Annaeus Seneca
(55 BC - AD 39). Roman rhetorician.

Shaw, George Bernard (1856-1950). Irish playwright, critic, social reformer.

Swift, Jonathan (1667-1745). English satirist.

Tennyson, Alfred, 1st Baron Tennyson (1809-1892). English poet.

Thoreau, Henry David (1817-1862). American essayist, naturalist, poet.

Tocqueville, Count Alexis de (1805-1859). French political leader, historian, writer.

Twain, Mark. Pen name of Samuel Langhorne Clemens (1835-1910). American writer and humorist.

Voltaire. Pen name of François Marie Arouet (1694-1778). French satirist, essayist, dramatist, philosopher, historian.

Whitehead, Alfred North (1861-1947). British philosopher, mathematician.

Wilde, Oscar (1854-1900). Irish-born English poet, playwright, novelist, wit.

Wotton, Sir Henry (1568-1639). English diplomat and poet.

Your Own Quotes

You may like to use this page to jot down some quotes
of your own - *bons mots* which you don't want to lose!